THE ROYAL HORTICULTURAL SOCIETY
PRACTICAL GUIDES

GRASSES &
BAMBOOS

THE ROYAL HORTICULTURAL SOCIETY
PRACTICAL GUIDES

GRASSES &
BAMBOOS

ROGER GROUNDS

DK

A Dorling Kindersley Book

LONDON, NEW YORK, MUNICH, MELBOURNE, DELHI

Project Editor Simon Maughan
Art Editor Ann Thompson

Series Art Editor Ursula Dawson

Managing Editor Anna Kruger
Managing Art Editor Lee Griffiths

DTP Designer Louise Waller

Production Manager Mandy Inness

First published in Great Britain in 2002
by Dorling Kindersley Limited,
80 Strand, London WC2R 0RL

A Penguin Company

A CIP catalogue for this book is available from the British Library.
ISBN 0 7513 37218

Reproduced by Colourscan, Singapore
Printed and bound by Star Standard Industries, Singapore

See our complete catalogue at
www.dk.com

CONTENTS

GRASSES IN THE GARDEN

WHAT ARE GRASSES?

LIKE LILIES AND ORCHIDS, grasses belong to a subdivision of the plant kingdom known as the monocots, in which the seedlings produce just one seed leaf. The grass family itself is the source of the grains that are the staff of life for most of mankind, and they provide the raw ingredients for bread, sugar, and alcohol, and serve as fodder for farm animals. It is one of the most fascinating families, showing endless diversity within the same essential architecture.

INTRODUCING THE FAMILY

Horticulturally, the term grasses is used to embrace not only the true grasses but also several other grass-like families, particularly sedges, rushes, and cat-tails. The bamboos are true grasses.

True grasses always have leaves that are flat, and stems that are cylindrical and hollow. By contrast, sedges have leaves and stems that are triangular in cross-section and solid. The leaves of the rushes arise straight from the ground and may be either cylindrical or flat. The cat-tail family is characterised by its strap-shaped leaves, presented in two clearly defined ranks, and characteristic female flowers that completely surround the strong, cylindrical flower stems, as exemplified by the common bulrush (*Typha latifolia*). Bamboos differ from other grasses in having woody stems or canes, which may branch, and leaves with stalks.

AUTUMN ADORNED
As summer shifts into autumn, grasses seem to dissolve or burn away as they catch the fiery tints of nearby deciduous trees and shrubs.

FROM FLUFFY FLOWERS TO LUSCIOUS LEAVES *Grasses offer an excess of fine foliage and flowers.*

WHY GROW GRASSES?

THE BEAUTY OF GRASSES is quite different from other garden plants. Rather than the static blobs of strong colour created by traditional flowers, grasses offer subtlety of line and texture, and a particular intimacy with the natural world. Their primary quality is their luminosity, the way they catch the light of the sky in their flowers and seedheads, drawing it into the garden. Then there is their transparency – the eye can see through them to other plants or features beyond.

MOVEMENT IN THE GARDEN

Grasses are never static. They ebb and flow through the seasons, burgeoning with abundant verdure in spring and maturing and flowering from summer onwards. In

> Grasses come alive in the breeze, appearing to dance in storms

autumn, they catch the orange, yellow, and red tints of that season, fading to mere ghosts of themselves in winter, often retaining their attractive seedheads. Their flowers metamorphose by gradual degrees into seedheads, and as these are dry structures, they can last for weeks or even months. Grasses stir with every slightest breeze and almost dance in storms. They even contribute sound to the garden; the leaves of some of the larger grasses rustle in the wind like a ball gown.

GRASSES ARE EASY TO GROW

Most grasses need little more than clean, weed-free earth to grow in, a site open to the sky, a little watering to get them

EXTENDING GRASSES TO THE MARGINS
There are many grasses, particularly sedges and rushes, that prefer moist or wet soil found at the margin of a pond or stream.

▲ BOLD STATEMENT
The feathery, fountain-shaped flowerheads of this tall eulalia grass (Miscanthus), *draw the eye to this border of large grasses.*

THE GREAT HEIGHTS OF GRASSES
Giant grasses can take the place of shrubs in a grass garden, dominating borders and forming boundaries along paths.

started, and some annual grooming. They are among the easiest of plants to grow well. Many are singularly drought-resistant once established, and providing they are not growing in too rich a soil, all except a few will keep competing weeds in check.

DIFFERENT SIZES AND SHAPES

Some of the smaller garden fescues grow to no more than 15cm (6in) tall, while at the other extreme there are monsters like the Provencal reed (*Arundo donax*), which grows to 4.2m (13ft). Some make tightly tufted little mounds, and there are types that form strong vertical uprights, fountain-shaped clumps or irregular drifts. Texture varies too, from fine, thread-like foliage to coarse, broad leaf blades. Sedges and rushes extend the range, providing species that will grow in shade and in damp conditions.

PRACTICAL CONSIDERATIONS

T HE SORTS OF PLANTS you can grow in your garden is determined chiefly by soil, climate and available sunlight. Most grasses, fortunately, are exceptionally tolerant of a wide range of climatic and cultural conditions, but they can be used to best effect if you are aware of their preferences. Give thought to where a grass will go in your garden when choosing and buying; for example, tall species suit the backs of borders and can act as boundaries or screens, and some spreading types are suitable for ground cover.

SUIT THE PLANTS TO THE SOIL

True grasses are mainly natives of poor ground and tend to grow out of character in heavily manured soils. The fertility of soil, therefore, is often reduced deliberately before planting grasses. This is achieved by increasing the mineral content of the soil, by digging in plenty of sand or grit (*see pp.48–49*). Sedges are an exception to this, and generally come from richer, damper soils, although woodrushes, which belong to the same family, are mostly woodland plants from poorer, drier soils. True rushes and cat-tails are really waterside plants, and prefer moist or wet, fertile soil.

SHADE OR SUN?

As a rule of thumb, true grasses grow best in full sun, while sedges and woodrushes prefer some shade at least. There are some exceptions, inevitably, but they are few. To be sure, always check the cultivation

▲ SHADES OF GREEN
Many foliage grasses thrive in shade, and their colours usually outlast flowering perennials, with their all-too-brief displays.

◄ WELCOME TO THE WATERSIDE
If you are lucky enough to have water in your garden, even a patch of boggy soil, you will be able to extend your planting palette.

▲ BAMBOO SCREEN
This colourful bamboo
(Phyllostachys aurea) *quickly*
forms an exceptionally pretty
screen or boundary.

◀ USE NATURAL LIGHT
Thoughtful positioning of
this oat grass (Stipa gigantea)
causes sunlight to illuminate
the flowerheads from behind.

requirements of a plant when you buy it, or ask for the advice of an experienced nurseryman. Alternatively, if you know the name of the plant, refer to pages 58–77.

In cool-temperate climates, most sun-loving grasses need to be in sun for at least half a day to perform well, but three to five hours sunshine may be sufficient in warmer areas. Given more sun, grasses will be stiffer and more erect; the more shade they have, the more their habit will be lax and they may flower less freely.

CLIMATE CONSIDERATIONS

Summer heat and winter cold limit the kinds of plants we can grow in our gardens. Most cool-season grasses – those that flower before midsummer – are very tolerant of cold, but intolerant of high temperatures. Conversely, most warm-season grasses, which flower after midsummer, need summer warmth to flower well, although most will withstand moderate frost.

> Most grasses prefer a site
> that receives full sun
> for at least half a day

Your garden is also likely to have several different microclimates, which will affect planting decisions. For example, if your garden faces the sun, it will be warmer and drier than a garden in shade for most of the day, and plants in the lee of a building will receive less rainfall than those in the open.

SOIL CONSIDERATIONS

THE TYPE OF SOIL YOU HAVE, whether clay, sand, or something in between, is determined by the size of the mineral particles in it. The two extremes are clay soils, made up of very fine particles, and sandy soils, which consist of large particles. You may have a mixture of the two, called loam. Soils can also be acid or alkaline. This is important if you want to grow rhododendrons or blue-flowered hydrangeas, but most grasses will grow in either type.

HOW TO TEST YOUR SOIL

In practice, the simplest way to tell which type of soil you have is to take a handful of it and roll it into a ball between your fingers. If, when you let go, the soil remains a compact ball, you have clay. If it fails to form a ball or it falls apart, then you have a sandy soil. If you are not clear which it has

done, you have a loamy soil. In some rare cases, more extreme soil types exist, and gardeners may need to seek specialist advice about these.

GRASSES AND SANDY SOILS

Sandy soils are usually poor in plant nutrients mainly because they drain quickly after rains, and any nutrients in the soil tend to be leached away quickly. While grasses on the whole like nutrient-poor soils, they need the presence of organic matter to maintain soil moisture levels. A yearly addition of organic matter – garden

GRASSES FOR SANDY SOILS

Calamagrostis × *acutiflora* 'Karl Foerster'
Dense, upright clumps, with feathery, purple-tinted flowerheads in early summer.
Holcus lanatus 'Variegatus' Low, creeping perennial with variegated foliage.
Spartina pectinata 'Aureomarginata' Tall, drift-forming grass with striped leaves.
Sporolobus heterolepis Low grass with fragrant flowerheads, ideal for ground cover.

SANDY BORDER DISPLAY
Sandy soils dry out and lose water and nutrients quickly. Improve growing conditions by adding organic matter to the soil.

DROUGHT-TOLERANT BORDER DISPLAY
Create a cool colour theme in a border with dry soil by mixing blue and silvery grasses with perennials of the same colour.

compost, for example – will help to hold nutrients in the soil, and the grasses will perform better as a result.

DEALING WITH DRY SOILS

Dry soil is a limiting factor in most gardens, but many grasses grow extremely well in such soils; their roots are singularly good at extracting water from apparently dry ground. Look for types with blue or grey leaves. These range from small blue fescues to large prairie grasses, such as switch grasses (*Panicum virgatum*) and Indian grass (*Sorghastrum avenaceum*), and include a number of first-rate flowering grasses like *Bouteloua gracilis*, fountain grasses (*Pennisetum*), *Helictotrichon sempervirens*, and feather grasses (*Stipa*).

Because of the paucity of water in dry soils, the plants need to be spaced well apart. Aesthetically, the best effects are

GRASSES FOR DRY SOILS

Andropogon gerardii Tall, upright blue-green grass that fades to orange and red in autumn.
Bouteloua gracilis Short, with curious flowers.
Festuca Small, colourful bun-shaped mounds.
Helictotrichon sempervirens Tall, silvery blue grass with arching flower stems.
Koeleria glauca Low blue, flowering mounds.
Leymus arenarius The most intense blue, but invasive, so it needs to be confined.
Melica altissima 'Atropurpurea' Tall purple flower spikes above floppy foliage.
Panicum virgatum Upright; many cultivars.
Pennisetum Fountain-like flowerheads.
Schizachyrium scoparium Blue-grey foliage that fades to orange-red in autumn.
Sorghastrum avenaceum 'Sioux Blue' Tall and upright with copper late summer flowerheads.
Stipa Fine grasses with feathery flowerheads.

often achieved by covering the ground with a mulch of pea-grit or slate fragments (*see p.52*), which has the additional benefit of inhibiting the growth of weeds and shading the soil, thereby helping to reduce evaporation from sunlight and wind.

IMPROVING CLAY SOILS

Clays are rich in plant nutrients, making them very fertile, but their stickiness and lack of aeration makes it difficult for plants to get established. They are also heavy and difficult to dig. Conditions for growing grasses can be greatly improved by the addition of bulky organic matter, as for sandy soils (*see pp.12–13*), and coarse, gritty sand in equal parts by volume, which will reduce the fertility of the soil (*see p.48*). These materials should be thoroughly mixed with the soil, not simply used as a mulch, although a layer of mulch will be helpful as well (*see p.52*).

GRASSES FOR CLAY SOILS

Calamagrostis × acutiflora 'Karl Foerster' Tall, dense tussocks with feathery flowerheads, lasting into winter. Also good in boggy soils.
Deschampsia cespitosa Clump-forming with tall flowerheads; popular, with many cultivars. Also good in boggy soils.
Elymus hispidus Eye-catching, with broad, electric-blue foliage and flowers.
Phalaris arundinacea var. *picta* Tall with striped leaves. Also good in boggy soils.

Clay soils are best dug in autumn and left over winter to weather. They should not be dug when wet, as this may cause severe damage to the soil structure.

WET OR BOGGY SOIL

Ground that is permanently damp provides an opportunity to grow a number of grasses and other plants to a degree of

> Extend your palette
> of grasses in an area
> of moist ground

vigour and luxuriance they will not attain in ordinary soil. The largest of these is the Provencal reed (*Arundo donax*), which can grow to 4.2m (13ft) tall with broad, blue-grey leaves. Most of the eulalia grasses (*Miscanthus sinensis*) and the moor grasses

CLAY-FIRED DISPLAY
Japanese blood grass (Imperata cylindrica 'Rubra'), *blue* Festuca glauca, *and ponytail grass* (Stipa tenuissima) *colour this display on clay.*

▲ FLOWER FOUNTAIN
*Creating the impression of a fountain,
gardeners' garters (*Phalaris arundinacea
var. *picta) is enhanced by the deep green,
umbrella-like leaves of* Gunnera manicata.

◄ MARGINAL HEIGHTS
*Tall species of moisture-loving grasses and
irises make good waterside companions.
Here, they confine and conceal a boggy pool.*

(*Molinia caerulea*) will flourish in these
conditions, as will a number of grasses with
brightly coloured leaves, especially Bowles'
golden sedge (*Carex elata* 'Aurea') and
striped ribbon grass (*Phalaris arundinacea*
var. *picta* 'Picta').

The qualities of these grasses can be
enhanced if they are grown among other
perennials with completely different sorts
of foliage, particularly ferns, astilbes,
and primulas. Tall species of grasses and
moisture-loving irises can be used to give
a design a focus point. Dense planting is
essential in moist ground to exclude weeds.

GRASSES FOR BOGGY SOILS

Arundo donax Very tall with blue-grey leaves.
Carex Sedges are grass-like perennials good
in damp, shady positions.
Cortaderia selloana Large and spectacular
pampas grass with feathery plumes.
Cyperus Distinctive foliage. Also good in
shallow water.
Luzula Low woodrushes that form good
ground cover.
Miscanthus sinensis Clump-forming with
pretty flowers and foliage. Many cultivars.
Molinia caerulea Lovely deciduous grasses.
Panicum virgatum 'Haense Herms' Cloud-like
flowers and orange-red foliage in autumn.
Spartina pectinata 'Aureomarginata' Clumps
of swaying, striped foliage and reddish flowers.

GRASSES FOR FLOWERS

THE BEAUTY OF FLOWERING GRASSES lies in their form and structure, rather than their colour, so the art of using them in the garden lies in contrasting these features, as you would have to do in a single-colour garden. The most important aspect of grasses is their ability to catch the light from the sky and hold it in their flowers. Because of this, they are best positioned where their flowerheads catch the sun, preferably against a dark background.

THE RANGE OF FLOWERS

Grasses are not usually grown for their individual flowers, more for their clusters of flowers or flowerheads. The flowers of *Stipa gigantea*, for example, are each over

> Plant a veil of see-through grasses in front of flowering perennials

5cm (2in) long, and these contrast with the tiny flowers of *Panicum virgatum*, but both are impressive because of the sheer numbers in which the flowers occur.

Flowerheads range in size from the huge plumes of pampas grasses (*Cortaderia*) to the small heads of *Melica uniflora*, and there are also great differences in transparency; those of some eulalia grasses (*Miscanthus sinensis*) are quite solid, while the flowerheads of tall moor grasses (*Molinia*) are quite translucent.

Very special effects can be created by using see-through grasses as a veil in front of more brightly coloured or substantial herbaceous perennials. For example, instead

CREATING CONTRASTS
This herbaceous border has it all, mixing different forms, textures, and colours. Notice how upright forms stop the eye.

MORE IDEAS

Calamagrostis Feathery flowerheads in early summer.
Deschampsia Cloud-like flowerheads in early summer.
Hordeum Barley flowerheads in midsummer.
Miscanthus Many-fingered plumes from midsummer.
Molinia Diffuse flowerheads from midsummer.
Panicum Clouds of flowers.
Pennisetum Feathery flowerheads in late summer.

◄ SMOKE AND FIRE
The solid, upright spikes of Eremurus × isabellinus *'Cleopatra' smoke like hot pokers amid* Stipa calamagrostis *and achilleas.*

▼ FLOWING FLOWERS
Grasses can create a feeling of ebb and flow, and planted among more static plants, like these flowering perennials, the effect is brought to the fore.

of banking the largest plants at the back and the smallest at the front, use some large grasses at the front and look through them to other plants beyond – through the flowers and stems of *Stipa gigantea*, perhaps, to a drift of daylilies beyond.

MIXING WITH PERENNIALS

When mixing grasses with perennials, try to group together that flower at the same time, using contrasting forms and colours. If *Kniphofia rooperi*, for example, with its solid spikes of vibrant orange, is grown with *Aster lateriflorus* 'Lady in Black', a wispy plant with mauve flowers, they will not only contrast harmoniously with each other, they will greatly add to the effectiveness of grasses also in flower, such as tall moor grasses, switch grasses (*Panicum virgatum*), and fountain grasses (*Pennisetum*).

GRASSES FOR FOLIAGE

I**T IS THE LINEARITY OF THEIR LEAVES** that makes grasses so distinct from other herbaceous perennials, and while the flowers of grasses occur within a narrow range of subtle shades, their foliage can be as bright as the gaudiest of bedding plants. The important thing to remember when combining grasses with colourful leaves is to ensure that all the grasses in any group have the same cultural requirements. Blue-leaved grasses, for example, often need drier conditions than white- or yellow-variegated grasses.

TYPES OF GRASS FOLIAGE

Quite the most spectacular foliage grass is Japanese blood grass (*Imperata cylindrica* 'Rubra') with perpendicular leaves that gradually become suffused with crimson. More useful are white-variegated types, like gardener's garters (*Phalaris arundinacea* var. *picta* 'Picta') and striped eulalia grass (*Miscanthus sinensis* 'Variegatus'), whose sheer whiteness draws the eye strongly. They can be placed to call attention to, or away from, particular parts of the garden. White-striped grasses are best planted, like flowering grasses, where they can be seen against a dark background with the sun beyond or beside them. Yellow-leaved or variegated grasses usually look better with the sun falling on them. Red- and yellow-leaved grasses are often effective grown in

association with blue-leaved grasses, which can be as small as the bun-shaped fescues (*Festuca*) or as large as *Panicum virgatum* 'Blue Tower', up to 2.7m (9ft) tall.

USING FOLIAGE TO FULL EFFECT

To create effective, contrasting displays, grow grasses with very narrow leaves, such as *Miscanthus sinensis* 'Gracillimus', next

FEATHERY FOIL
Golden Carex elata *'Aurea' contrasts cleverly with blue* Elymus magellanicus, Stipa pennata *and bright red crocosmia flowers.*

MORE SUGGESTIONS

Calamagrostis × *acutiflora* 'Overdam'
White-striped foliage, graceful in the breeze.
Carex oshimensis 'Evergold' Creamy leaves
Elymus hispidus Bright blue foliage.
Glyceria maxima var. *variegata* Cream-striped leaves, most conspicuous in spring.
Leymus arenarius Intense blue foliage.
Luzula sylvatica 'Aurea' Golden leaves.
Molinia caerulea subsp. *caerulea* 'Variegata'
Dramatically cream-striped all over.
Phalaris arundinacea var. *picta* Variegated grasses; 'Picta' and 'Feesey' are popular.
Schizachyrium scoparium Blue foliage turns orange-red in autumn; useful in winter.
Uncinia rubra Red to brownish foliage, depending on the amount of light.

▲ TEXTURAL EFFECTS
The sharp geometry of this summer house is offset by a round, shrubby euphorbia and bamboos and grasses with fine, colourful foliage.

◄ COLOUR CONTRASTS
Hakonechloa macra 'Aureola' *is a fine foliage grass with many colourful cultivars. They form mounds of cascading leaves, which take on wine-red hues from late summer.*

to those with bold, broad foliage, like the Provencal reed (*Arundo donax*). Alternatively, grow grasses with perennials or shrubs with completely different leaves, *Bergenia cordifolia*, for example, whose

---

Bright grasses will draw the eye to particular parts of the garden

---

leaves are almost round. Contrasting foliage, however, does not have to be bold. The coarse, dock-like leaves of *Silphium terebinthinaceum* are always held erect, contrasting well with pampas grasses (*Cortaderia*) or cascading bamboos like

Fargesia murielae. Sometimes colour can come into the equation too; the furry leaves of *Stachys byzantina* or the larger, smoother leaves of *Verbascum bombyciferum* blend well with the silvery blue *Helictotrichon sempervirens* or *Festuca glauca* 'Elijah Blue', also providing a contrast in shape.

Further effects can be achieved by having larger, single specimen grasses spring up through carpets of lower-growing grasses (*see pp.22–23*). Any of the tall moor grasses (*Molinia*) or medium to large eulalia grasses (*Miscanthus sinensis*) might be used as specimens amid drifts of *Hakonechloa macra* or *Festuca glauca* or, on a larger scale, the light-green-leaved *Cortaderia richardii* among a dark-leaved drift of *Deschampsia cespitosa*.

MEADOWS AND WILDFLOWER LAWNS

GARDENING WITH WILD FLOWERS often stems from a wish to conserve native species, and growing even a small area of wild plants in a lawn or meadow contributes to their conservation and attracts a variety of insects (often beneficial) and other wildlife into the garden. The growing conditions will determine the plants that thrive and look natural in the setting, but remember to keep the emphasis on the massed effect rather than individual plants.

MAKING MEADOWS

By definition, lawns and meadows are mown, but the frequency of mowing determines the quantities of wild flowers that grow among the grasses. The less often mown, the more wild flowers will appear.

> Wildflower lawns often look tidier if surrounded by a mown border

Wildflower lawns can be created quite simply by reducing mowing, making the first cut in midsummer, and keeping the grass down to about 10cm (4in) until early autumn, when the autumn crocuses appear. Even traditional lawns, if not treated with chemicals, contain daisies, buttercups, self-heal, hawkbit, and often cowslips and primroses, these will quickly come to the fore if the grass is allowed to grow. They can be supplemented with further native wild flowers, which can be bought as plug plants and slipped in among the grasses. In small gardens, wildflower lawns look best if they are contained within a strip of mown grass around the edges.

MEADOW IN FLOWER
A wildflower lawn in full bloom not only provides an attractive display, it is also a rich source of nectar for bees and butterflies.

▲ MIXING IT UP
Remember that grasses are wild flowers in their own right, forming the backbone to any meadow planting. The subtle texture and colour of their flowerheads mix well with more showy flowers.

▶ WILD WONDERLAND
An open, sunny site is ideal for a wildflower meadow, maybe in a part of the garden that is seen but rarely used. Trees can be used to punctuate or add interest to large drifts of wild flowers.

Meadows are similar but generally larger and made of taller grasses and wild flowers. They are mown less frequently, in early summer and autumn only.

INTRODUCING WILD GARDENS

Wild gardens look wild, even though they are not. The essence is to plant exotic or cultivated species in a matrix of wild, native vegetation, and plants in the tapestry are then left to sustain themselves, without further interference. In such a scheme, the individual plants assume more importance than in wildflower meadows or lawns.

In a typical wild garden, you might see large plants like red-hot pokers or cow parsley, coarse grasses like *Cortaderia selloana*, larger eulalia grasses (*Miscanthus sinensis*), or drifts of autumn crocuses naturalized in areas of short turf.

SPECIMEN GRASSES

MOST GRASSES LOOK BEST when grown in groups or drifts, but many are also excellent specimens – plants that are grown on their own or set into a border in a focal position, where their unique qualities are revealed to best effect. Specimen grasses will draw the eye strongly, so they can be used to direct attention towards particular parts of the garden or away from less desirable areas. They may even be used to hide unsightly objects, such as a shed or compost bin.

BEYOND PAMPAS GRASS

The strong shape and tall, graceful plumes of pampas grass (*Cortaderia selloana*) is probably the first thing that comes to mind when specimen grasses are mentioned, although there is much more to the subject than just this one plant. Large grasses like the provencal reed (*Arundo donax*), and the larger eulalia grasses (*Miscanthus sinensis*) all make excellent specimens, as do bamboos like *Fargesia murielae* and *Phyllostachys bambusoides* 'Castillonis'.

Tall specimens are often grown in small island beds in a lawn, while smaller types, such as maiden grass (*Miscanthus sinensis* 'Gracillimus') and fountain grass (*Pennisetum*

AUTUMN ACTION
The feathery nature of these tall flowerheads not only catches the eye, but they also emphasize the shape of surrounding plants.

alopecuroides), can be grown in gravel beds set into paved areas. Many can be treated as specimens if grown in large containers and sited where they will catch the eye. Sedges, such as *Carex oshimensis* 'Evergold'

> Specimen grasses are on show at all times, so keep them well groomed

and *C. testacea*, can be used this way, as can Hakone grass (*Hakonechloa macra*).

The most important single consideration with specimen grasses is that they must look good at all times. This means paying attention to their feeding, watering, and annual grooming (*see p.53*). Withered leaves or broken canes left on the plant will mar its appearance.

SOME SUGGESTIONS

Arundo donax Very tall, blue-grey grass.
Chusquea couleou Tall, arching bamboo.
Cortaderia Large and spectacular pampas grasses with narrow leaves and silky plumes.
Fargesia Elegant bamboos, colourful canes.
Hakonechloa macra '**Alboaurea**' Golden form of Hakone grass, good in a container.
Miscanthus sinensis Good cultivars include 'Strictus' and var. *condensatus* 'Cosmopolitan'.
Pennisetum alopecuroides Shorter type.
Phyllostachys bambusoides 'Castillonis' Bamboo with very colourful canes.
Phyllostachys nigra Bamboo with black canes.
Semiarundinaria fastuosa Upright bamboo.
Stipa gigantea Tall, feathery flowerheads.

◀ EXCLAMATION MARK
Strongly upright plants make the eye pause; Miscanthus sinensis *'Morning Light' brings a focus to this colourful planting.*

▼ JOLLY GREEN GIANT
The weeping foliage of this tall eulalia grass (Miscanthus sinensis), *catches the light and points down to the mixed planting below.*

BAMBOOS IN THE GARDEN

S OUND AND MOVEMENT ARE TWO of the major contributions that bamboos
make to a garden. The leaves rustle mysteriously with every breath of wind
and sway gracefully with every gust. The largest bamboos also make elegant,
shuttlecock-shaped clumps with shining, often brightly coloured canes topped
with tumbling foliage. The smallest bamboos make miniature groves of grassy
green leaves – these are best confined to containers as their roots run vigorously.

GIANT AND DWARF BAMBOOS

Bamboos range in size from giants like
Phyllostachys edulis, reaching 20m (70ft)
even in quite cool climates, to miniatures
like *Pleioblastus akebono*, growing to no
more than 30cm (12in) tall. Between these
extremes lie a vast variety of types, some
with coloured canes, others with variegated
foliage. Most bamboos, however, are
valued purely for their quiet greenery.

Tall bamboos have a tree-like appearance
and are most often seen growing as isolated
specimens in lawns; clump-forming species
with cascading foliage, such as *Chusquea
culeou* and *Thamnocalamus crassinodus*
suit this purpose. Many also make excellent
hedges or screens, needing no trimming
beyond the routine removal of dead

canes. Among the best for hedging are
Phyllostachys bissetii, which stays fresh
and green in winter, *Fargesia nitida* and
F. murielae, *Pseudosasa japonica*, and

> ## With palm-like companions, bamboos create a tropical effect

Pleioblastus simonii. Bamboos, being
shallow rooted, can be used near buildings.

MANY LEVELS OF PLANTING
*Bamboos draw the eye to the sky. Keep the
emphasis in the garden using attractive ground
cover, like this miniature rhododendron.*

Phyllostachys aureosulcata 'Aureocaulis' and 'Spectabilis' Tall and clump-forming cultivars with yellow canes.
Phyllostachys bambusoides 'Castillonis' Tall with very colourful golden yellow canes.
Phyllostachys nigra Tall with green canes that mature to a solid, shining black.
Pleioblastus auricomus Tall with purplish canes and dramatically striped foliage.
Pleioblastus variegatus Shorter bamboo to 1.5m (5ft) with variegated foliage.
Semiarundinaria fastuosa Tall and stately, with green then purplish canes.

◄ GOLDEN RODS
A quiet corner of leafy greenery is illuminated by the canes and tumbling foliage of Phyllostachys vivax.

▼ SILHOUETTES IN SILVER POTS
Patio and courtyard gardens make ideal homes for bamboos. They suit modern architecture and they bring an exotic feel.

In the gardens of town houses, a single large bamboo, with only its showiest canes retained, can be used to create the effect of an Oriental courtyard. Associated with the palms *Butia capitata*, *Chamaerops humilis*, and *Trachycarpus fortunei*, Japanese banana (*Musa basjoo*), and ginger lilies (*Hedychium*), bamboos give a tropical effect.

Cultivating Bamboos

While most ornamental grasses do best in poor soils, bamboos give rich rewards for good cultivation. Their basic requirements are shelter from strong winds and good soil drainage. Being shallow-rooted, they also need moisture-retentive soil, and they benefit greatly from mulches of organic materials. Given these and a modicum of encouragement, a bamboo will grow to its full height in just a few years.

RUSHES AND SEDGES

ALTHOUGH THEY ARE SEPARATED from the true grasses by billions of years of evolution, rushes and sedges have a superficial similarity to grasses, and their fondness for damp and shady places therefore extends the range of grass-like plants into these parts of the garden. Generally, the sedges make arching tufts of basal leaves, although a few have a running habit, while the rushes are little more than bundles of hollow, cylindrical stems.

COMPARING RUSHES AND SEDGES

Sedges are a much smaller group of plants than the grasses. They are mostly quite small plants under 30cm (12in) tall, and they grow best in shadier and damper situations, with the variegated varieties excelling in shade. The rushes make an even smaller group and are true moisture-lovers; they will only flourish in wet ground or with their feet in water. As a consequence, rushes are usually planted at the edges of ponds, pools, or lakes, where their vertical appearance contrasts with the horizontal line of the water.

Sedges are mainly grown for their foliage, which is often stiffer than that of grasses and evergreen. Their flowers are also quite different, and while interesting, they lack

> Rushes are waterside plants, flourishing with their feet in water

the airy grace of the true grasses. They are useful in shaded parts of the garden, where the true grasses will not grow well.

▲ RANGE OF COLOUR
These two popular sedges, Carex comans *bronze and* C. ornithopoda *'Variegata', show off their coloured and variegated foliage.*

▶ SEDGE IN THE BORDER
Bowles' golden sedge, Carex elata *'Aurea', excels as a bright foliage perennial, highlighted by the dark hedge beyond.*

EFFECTIVE DESIGNS

Some sedges – many from New Zealand – can actually be described as sun-lovers. They are ideal in bold, weed-proof groups of bronze, white or green, punctuated with compatriots grown as specimen plants, such as cordylines and leptospermums.

Most of the favourite shade-loving sedges have coloured or variegated foliage and associate well with ferns, hellebores, pulmonarias, ivies, and bamboos. They can be massed as ground cover, or used singly to give continuity between flowering plants.

Rushes are usually used as single specimens in or at the edge of water. Choose good garden varieties, such as club-rush (*Schoenoplectus*) or corkscrew rush (*Juncus effusus* 'Spiralis'), since rushes have overtones poor husbandry; many are weedy plants of badly drained soil.

▶ DWARF REEDMACE
This manageable species of reedmace, Typha minima, *is the only type suitable for a small pond. Its flowerheads are good for cutting.*

▲ STRIPY CLUB-RUSH
Schoenoplectus lacustris *subsp.* lacustris tabernaemontani *'Zebrinus' is a lovely striped form of club-rush.*

RECOMMENDATIONS

Carex berggrenii Silvery brown foliage.
C. buchananii Rolled leaves with pig-tail curls.
C. comans Several colourful cultivars.
C. elata '**Aurea**' Arching yellow, striped leaves.
C. grayi Spiky, club-like flowerheads good for indoor flower arrangements.
C. morrowii '**Variegata**' White-striped foliage; 'Fisher's Form' has cream stripes.
C. muskingumensis Yellowish foliage; 'Oehme' has gold-edged leaves.
C. oshimensis '**Evergold**' Cream-green leaves.
C. petriei Pale, pinkish brown foliage.
C. siderosticha '**Variegata**' White-striped form.
Juncus decipiens '**Curly-wurly**' Rush with tightly twisted green stems, like wire wool; *J. inflexus* 'Afro' is similar but grey-green.
Schoenoplectus lacustris subsp. *tabernae-montani* For wet soils or water. 'Albescens' has white stems, 'Zebrinus' is striped.

EXTENDING THE DISPLAY

WHILE ORNAMENTAL GRASSES WERE originally introduced to gardens to extend the floral display beyond that achieved by traditional herbaceous perennials alone, it is a paradox that their main flowering season is limited between midsummer and late autumn. Grasses themselves, therefore, benefit from association with perennials performing both earlier and later in the year. Proximity to hedges and geometric topiary also extends their season of interest.

GOING TO SEED

The reason why grasses have such a long season of interest, which extends well into autumn, is that their late summer flowers quickly turn to seedheads. Being dry, these can last for several months. Most grasses, therefore, look good not only through late summer and autumn, but also through much of winter as well.

In winter, the effectiveness of grass seedheads can be greatly enhanced if they are grown with other herbaceous perennials whose seedheads or winter skeletons are also interesting, often contrasting in shape with the grasses. Among the best of these are many umbellifers, including fennel (*Foeniculum vulgare*), Queen Anne's lace (*Anthriscus sylvestris*), giant angelica (*Angelica gigas*), wood angelica (*Angelica sylvestris*), and Himalayan cow parsley (*Selinum wallichianum*), as well as several daisies like *Coreopsis verticillata*, assorted heleniums, black-eyed Susan (*Rudbeckia fulgida* 'Goldsturm' and *R. maxima*), and

SNOWY SEEDHEADS
The classic plumes of pampas grass are strong and weather-resistant, lasting well in winter. Remove broken canes to maintain the display.

WINTER SEEDHEADS

Calamagrostis brachytricha Red seedheads.
Miscanthus sinensis Plume-like seedheads.
Molinia caerulea Feathery seedheads.
Panicum virgatum Cloud-like seedheads.
Pennisetum alopecuroides Tail-like seedheads.
Phalaris arundinacea Upright seedheads.
Spartina pectinata 'Aureomarginata' Reddish brown seedheads.
Spodiopogon sibiricus Greyish seedheads.
Stipa arundinacea Feathery seedheads.

varieties of New England aster (*Aster novae-angliae*). Other useful perennials include *Phlomis samia*, Joe Pye weeds (*Eupatorium purpureum*), ice plants (*Sedum spectabile*), and varieties of *Veronicastrum virginicum*.

A SPRING LAUNCH

The disadvantage of grasses performing for such a long season is that they have to be cut down just as spring arrives. This is an essential, late winter job, which will make

way for the next season's growth. In gardens with a lot of grasses, cutting back can leave large areas of bare earth, and the remedy here is to establish spring bulbs

The dry seedheads of grasses can last for weeks or even months

under the grasses, trying to keep the vigour of the bulbs proportional to the vigour of the grasses among which they are planted. Spring bulbs should be planted in autumn.

The season can start in late winter with snowdrops, for example, and then continue into spring with an assortment of crocuses. These can be followed by early then late daffodils, and then by tulips. Finally, the tall, upright spikes of camassias can follow, whose flowering will end just as the first of the early-flowering grasses, such as *Stipa gigantea*, launch themselves into flower.

SPACE FOR SPRING BULBS
There is a gap that needs filling in the grass calendar in spring, so interplant them with seasonal bulbs, like these dark-flowered tulips.

GOOD COMPANIONS

Bergenia Many types with pink spring flowers and evergreen, paddle-shaped leaves.
Camassia quamash Bright blue, spire-like flowerheads in late spring.
Cimicifuga White, upright spikes in autumn.
Echinacea purpureum Purple daisy flowers in late summer and autumn.
Lavandula Fragrant shrubby evergreens with mauve flowerheads through summer.
Liriope muscari Violet spikes in autumn amid broad, grass-like, evergreens foliage.
Perovskia 'Blue Spire' Small silvery shrub with violet, late summer and autumn flowers.
Sedum 'Herbsfreude' (syn. S. Autumn Joy) Flat, pinkish flowerheads in autumn.
× *Solidaster* Yellow, daisy-like flowerheads from midsummer to early autumn.
Verbascum Tall summer spires of usually yellow flowers amid silvery foliage.

PLANTING PLANS AND SCHEMES

CHOOSING A PLANTING STYLE

THE KEY TO GOOD PLANTING DESIGN is to ensure that the plants are well-suited to the soil and growing conditions, and it certainly helps if all the plants in any one grouping share the same environmental preferences. Begin by identifying the situation in which you want to grow a grass display – is it shady or sunny, wet or dry? – and use the ideas on the following pages to help you choose a scheme to suit the individual requirements of your own garden.

GRASS AND BAMBOO BORDERS

When grasses are used in traditional garden schemes, they are generally dotted around or among more prominent shrubs or herbaceous perennials. With the growing interest in grasses, however, they are being used more and more in borders composed wholly of grasses or where grasses are the dominant feature. In these modern garden designs, it is the contrasting shapes, forms, and textures of the grasses that matter; colour is very much a secondary consideration. Probably, the best balance between grasses and other perennials is achieved when a planting is made up of about one-fifth grasses, these being chosen mainly to extend the season of interest beyond midsummer (*see pp.28–29*).

QUIET CHORUS
Shapes, forms, and textures dominate this grass-only border as they sway and intermingle with the flow of the breeze.

BALANCING ACT Stipa tenuissima *mingles with the red flowers of* Knautia macedonica.

PLANTING FOR COLOUR

Grasses with coloured foliage can be used to create effects every bit as bright as summer bedding. For the finest effects, use several plants of the same type to make an informal group or drift, and position this next to groups of different colours. Colourful grasses look best with the sun beyond or beside them. This planting is shown at its peak in late summer.

Miscanthus sinensis 'Variegatus' Tall grass making a rounded or upright clump with striking, white-variegated leaves.

Cortaderia selloana 'Aureolineata' Yellow-edged leaves topped by plumes in autumn.

Panicum virgatum 'Blue Tower' Arching, grey-blue foliage – a superb foil for other colours.

Miscanthus sinensis 'Goldfeder' Arching leaves with broad, bright yellow edges.

Spartina pectinata 'Aureomarginata' Loose drifts of yellow-edged leaves that sway gently in the wind.

Chionochloa rubra Tall clumps of foxy-red leaves, most intense in winter.

Phalaris arundinacea var. *picta* 'Feesey' Bright, white-variegated leaves tinged pink in spring.

Alopecurus pratensis 'Aureovariegatus' Rich yellow leaves striped with green. Foxtail-like flowers.

Calamagrostis × *acutiflora* 'Overdam' Dense tufts of white-striped leaves tinged pink in spring.

Phormium tenax **Purpureum Group** Introduces a striking architectural element.

HELICTOTRICHON
SEMPERVIRENS
*Blue oat grass bears its
straw-coloured flowerheads
on slender, arching stems.*

PLANTING PLAN

1 *Miscanthus sinensis* 'Variegatus', 1.8m (6ft) tall
2 *Cortaderia selloana* 'Aureolineata', 1.7m (5½ft) tall
3 *Chionochloa rubra*, 1.5m (5ft) tall
4 *Miscanthus sinensis* 'Goldfeder', 2m (6ft) tall
5 *Spartina pectinata* 'Aureomarginata', 1.7m (5½ft) tall
6 *Panicum virgatum* 'Blue Tower', 1.8m (6ft) tall
7 *Carex buchananii*, 50cm (20in) tall
8 *Festuca glauca* 'Elijah Blue', 30cm (12in) tall
9 *Imperata cylindrica* 'Rubra', 30cm (12in) tall
10 *Hakonechloa macra* 'Alboaurea', 30cm (12in) tall
11 *Helictotrichon sempervirens*, 1.2m (4ft) tall
12 *Alopecurus pratensis* 'Aureovariegatus', 30cm (12in) tall
13 *Calamagrostis* × *acutiflora* 'Overdam', 1.8m (6ft) tall
14 *Phormium tenax* Purpureum Group, 2.4m (8ft) tall
15 *Phalaris arundinacea* var. *picta* 'Feesey', 1.5m (5ft) tall

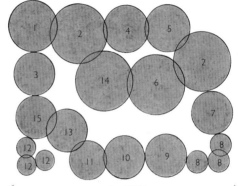

2.2m (7ft)

3m (10ft)

Carex buchananii Small
sedge with a good
strong foxy-red colour
all year round.

MORE CHOICES

Glyceria maxima var.
variegata
Hakonechloa macra
'Aureola' and
'Mediovariegata'
Holcus mollis
'Albovariegatus'
Miscanthus sinensis
'Dixieland' and 'Strictus'
Phalaris arundincea var.
picta 'Luteopicta'
Sorghastrum nutans
'Sioux Blue'

konechloa macra
boaurea' Drifts
arching, golden
low leaves.

Imperata cylindrica
'Rubra' Red-tipped
leaves in spring
become wholly blood-
red by midsummer.

Festuca glauca 'Elijah
Blue' Strong blue
foliage. Grows best
in sandy or gritty soil.

GRAVEL GARDENS

This type of garden is most successful in the sunniest, best-drained part of the garden. Dig in the gravel to a depth of 30–45cm (12–18in) to ensure sharp drainage and to impoverish the soil (see p.48). Grasses and other perennials suited to gravel gardens will flop and fail in rich, well-fed soils. Plenty of gravel should be visible between the plants, shown here in midsummer.

PLANTING PLAN

1 Three large, rugged rocks
2 Gravel pathway, leading eye to rocks
3 *Panicum virgatum* 'Prairie Sky', 90cm (36in) tall
4 *Stipa gigantea*, 1.8m (6ft) tall
5 *Festuca glauca* 'Elijah Blue', 30cm (12in) tall
6 *Salvia × superba*, 60cm (24in) tall
7 *Helictotrichon sempervirens*, 90cm (36in) tall
8 *Perovskia* 'Blue Spire', 1.2m (4ft) tall
9 *Limonium platyphyllum*, 75cm (30in) tall
10 *Coreopsis verticillata* 'Moonbeam', 50cm (20in) tall, interplanted with *Allium giganteum*, 1.8m (6ft) tall
11 *Yucca filamentosa*, 75cm (30in) tall
12 *Pennisetum orientale*, 90cm (36in) tall

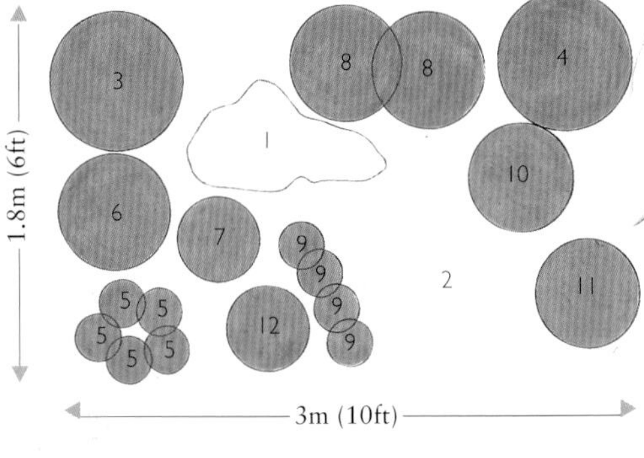

Panicum virgatum 'Prairie Sky'
Powdery blue all over; best in poor, well-drained soil in full sun.

Helictotrichon sempervirens Look like a fibre-optic to with narrow, steel blue-grey leaves.

1.8m (6ft)

3m (10ft)

Salvia × superba
Intense indigo flower spikes, best from midsummer to autumn.

FESTUCA GLAUCA 'ELIJAH BLUE'
This is the largest of the little blue fescues with rich, silvery blue leaves, stems, and flowers. The colour is less intense in winter.

Perovskia 'Blue Spire'
Wispy, fragrant and
feathery, silver leaves.
Spires of blue flowers
from midsummer.

Stipa gigantea Low
mounds of dark,
evergreen leaves
with tall wands
of golden flowers
from early summer.

Allium giganteum
Ornamental onion
topped with tennis-
ball-sized heads of
pink-purple flowers.

Coreopsis verticillata
'Moonbeam' Covered
by starry, pale yellow
daisies in late summer.

Yucca filamentosa
Grown mainly for
the strong succulent
rosettes, made up
of thick, silver-grey,
sword-shaped leaves.

Limonium platyphyllum
Large, branching
heads of tiny purple-
blue flowers, which
last for months; they
are lovely for picking
and drying.

Pennisetum orientale
Forms a neat,
rounded clump with
fluffy flower spikes.

CONTAINER GARDENS

For a good-looking container display, shown here in midsummer, choose containers that compliment the foliage of the grasses and are large and deep enough to allow the roots to develop.

Try to stick to the same style of pot within a group, and site them in a sheltered position in sun or part-day shade. Remember to keep the soil reasonably moist at all times.

Carex comans bronze
Similar to *Carex* 'Frosted Curls' but foxy-red in colour. It also needs to be elevated.

Imperata cylindrica
'Rubra' Blood-red foliage that is best with the sun behind it so the sun shines through. It needs adequate moisture.

PLANTING PLAN

1 *Miscanthus sinensis* 'Morning Light', 1.5m (5ft) tall
2 *Carex comans* 'Frosted Curls', 45cm (18in) tall
3 *Carex comans* bronze, 45cm (18in) tall
4 *Imperata cylindrica* 'Rubra', 30cm (12in) tall
5 *Hakonechloa macra* 'Alboaurea', 23cm (9in) tall
6 *Helictotrichon sempervirens*, 90cm (36in) tall
7 *Pennisetum villosum*, 60cm (24in) tall

MORE CHOICES

Carex oshimensis 'Evergold'
Carex pendula
Festuca
Juncus
Leymus arenarius
Molinia caerulea
   'Variegata'
Pennisetum setaceum
   'Rubrum'
Phalaris arundinacea
   var. *picta*
Phyllostachys nigra
Sasa veitchii
Typha minima

Miscanthus sinensis
'**Morning Light**' Forms
mushroom-shaped clumps
of very narrow, white-
edged leaves. It is ideal
for large containers.

Helictotrichon sempervirens
The symmetrical outline
with radiating, bluish leaves
compliments terracotta
pots perfectly.

Carex comans '**Frosted
Curls**' Makes clumps of
long, whitish-green, hair-like
leaves that spread over the
sides of the pot, hanging
vertically downwards. The
pot needs to be elevated
to cascade well.

Hakonechloa macra
'**Alboaurea**' Forms mounds
of cascading foliage that
turns to red in autumn.

Pennisetum villosum
Produces a continuous
display of fluffy, almost
white flowers from early
summer until the first frosts.
It has a slightly spreading
shape, wider than it is tall.

SHADED AREAS

Many grasses tolerate shade, even those that are considered sun-lovers; these may take on unusual growth forms in shade, such as *Calamagrostis* × *acutiflora* 'Karl Foerster' – upright in sun, but gently arching in shade. Then there are those types that thrive in shade only. Varieties with bright foliage will illuminate a shaded area. This display is shown in late summer.

Fargesia murielae
Forms a fountain-shaped mound with soft green foliage.

Calamagrosti *brachytricha*
Pinkish-mauv flowerheads and lax habi

Spodiopogon sibiricus
Silver-purple flowers followed by good autumn colour.

Hakonechloa macra 'Alboaurea' Arching mounds of yellow and green leaves. It tolerates all but the driest shade.

Luzula sylvatica 'Aurea' Brilliant yellow, ground-covering woodrush.

Chasmanthium latifolium Hanging flowers like flattened lockets. Best grown in drifts.

Poa colensoi An unusual colour for a shade-loving grass.

Calamagrostis × acutiflora 'Karl Foerster' Vertical in sun, it arches gently in shade.

Deschampsia cespitosa **'Goldschleier'** Tufts of dark, evergreen leaves and acid-yellow flowers.

Molinia caerulea susbp. *arundinacea* **'Bergfreund'** Cloud-like plumes of tiny grey flowers. Leaves turn butter-yellow in autumn.

PLANTING PLAN

1 *Fargesia murielae*, 3.6m (11ft) tall
2 *Luzula sylvatica* 'Aurea', 45cm (18in) tall
3 *Calamagrostis* × *acutiflora* 'Karl Foerster', 1.5m (5ft) tall
4 *Molinia caerulea* subsp. *arundinacea* 'Bergfreund', 1.8m (6ft) tall
5 *Pleioblastus variegatus* 'Tsuboii', 1.2m (4ft) tall
6 *Deschampsia cespitosa* 'Goldschleier', 1.2m (4ft) tall
7 *Carex oshimensis* 'Evergold', 45cm (18in) tall
8 *Milium effusum* 'Aureum' × 5, 30cm (12in) tall
9 *Hakonechloa macra* 'Alboaurea', 23cm (9in) tall
10 *Spodiopogon sibiricus*, 1.2m (4ft) tall
11 *Calamagrostis brachytricha*, 1.2m (4ft) tall
12 *Chasmanthium latifolium*, 60cm (24in) tall
13 *Poa colensoi* × 3, 30cm (12in) tall

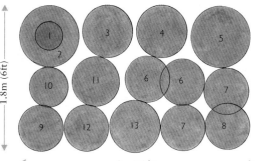

Pleioblastus variegatus **'Tsuboii'** Bright, white-variegated bamboo that that draws the eye into the shaded area. It scorches in full sun.

Carex oshimensis **'Evergold'** Evergreen mounds of shiny, creamy yellow leaves edged with dark green.

Milium effusum **'Aureum'** The whole plant is soft yellow in early summer.

MORE CHOICES

Calamagrostis brachytricha
Carex morrowii 'Variegata'
Carex pendula
Chimonobambusa marmorea
Chusquea culeou
Fargesia nitida
Hakonechloa macra
Imperata cylindrica
Luzula sylvatica 'Hohe Tatra' and 'Marginata'
Melica uniflora
Phyllostachys aurea
Pleioblastus auricomus
Sasa veitchii
Semiarundinaria fastuosa
Uncinia rubra

PONDS AND WATERSIDE

This amphitheatre-like water feature, shown in midsummer, forms a stage of slender grasses and flowering perennials framed by a backdrop of tall grasses. The vertical aspect of grasses works well with the horizontal surface of the water. Bold and narrow foliage create a contrast of texture, and the flowering perennials give a liberal splash of colour.

Arundo donax Strongly upright with very broad, grey-green leaves.

Miscanthus × *giganteus* Lush foliage gives a subtropical look.

Astilbe 'Bressingham Beauty' Ferny foliage and bright pink, fluffy flowers in large heads.

Ligularia dentata 'Desdemona' Large, round leaves and bright orange daisy flowers.

Schoenoplectus lacustris subsp. *tabernaemontani* 'Zebrinus' Stripy, upright stems.

Juncus effusus f. *spiralis* Rush with corkscrew-like stems.

PLANTING PLAN

1 *Arundo donax*, 4.5m (13½ft) tall
2 *Miscanthus × giganteus*, 3.3m (10½ft) tall
3 *Miscanthus sinensis* 'Variegatus', 1.5m (5ft) tall
4 *Miscanthus sinensis* 'China', 1.5m (5ft) tall
5 *Ligularia dentata* 'Desdemona', 1m (3ft) tall
6 *Astilbe* 'Bressingham Beauty', 1.2m (4ft) tall
7 *Glyceria maxima* var. *variegata*, 1.8m (6ft) tall
8 *Juncus effusus* f. *spiralis*, 30cm (12in) tall
9 *Acorus calamus* 'Argenteostriatus', 90cm (36in) tall
10 *Schoenoplectus lacustris* subsp. *tabernaemontani* 'Zebrinus', 1.5m (5ft) tall
11 *Zantedeschia aethiopica* 'Crowborough', 90cm (36in) tall
12 *Typha minima*, 65cm (26in) tall

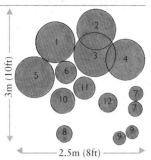

3m (10ft)

2.5m (8ft)

Miscanthus sinensis 'China'
Red-wine flowers in midsummer that fade to silver then buff. Grown for its flowers rather than its foliage.

MISCANTHUS SINENSIS 'VARIEGATUS'
This variegated eulalia grass with abundant lush foliage gives a subtropical look.

Zantedeschia aethiopica 'Crowborough' Large white spathes above dark green leaves.

Typha minima
The daintiest of the bulrushes, for wet ground or water.

MORE CHOICES

Carex pendula
Carex riparia 'Variegata'
Cyperus longus
Eriophorum angustifolium
Imperata cylindrica 'Rubra'
Juncus inflexus 'Afro'
Phragmites australis 'Variegatus'
Schoenoplectus lacustris subsp. *tabernaemontani* 'Golden Spear'
Typha angustifolia
Typha latifolia 'Variegata'

Glyceria maxima var. variegata Variegated foliage that is bright pink when young, fading to cream.

Acorus calamus 'Argenteostriatus' Bold, iris-like, white-striped foliage.

YEAR-ROUND INTEREST

Although summer is the main season of interest for grasses, their flowerheads quickly dry out to form attractive seedheads. Many of these persist through winter, and their beauty is increased if associated with other plants whose winter skeletons are also interesting. Displays can be improved early in the year with spring flowers (*see box*). This border is shown in late summer.

PLANTING PLAN

1 *Phyllostachys aureosulcata* 'Aureocaulis', 3.5m (11ft) tall
2 *Calamagrostis × acutiflora* 'Karl Foerster', 1.5m (5ft) tall
3 *Cortaderia selloana* 'Pumila', 1.5m (5ft) tall
4 *Stipa gigantea*, 1.8m (6ft) tall
5 *Miscanthus sinensis* 'Ferner Osten', 1.2m (4ft) tall
6 *Eupatorium purpureum* 'Gateway', 1.8m (6ft) tall
7 *Lythrum virgatum* 'Dropmore Purple', 1.2m (4ft) tall
8 *Panicum virgatum* 'Blue Tower', 2.7m (9ft) tall
9 *Perovskia* 'Blue Spire', 1.2m (4ft) tall
10 *Liatris spicata*, 90cm (36in) tall
11 *Carex petriei* × 2, 30cm (12in) tall
12 *Rudbeckia fulgida* 'Goldsturm', 60cm (24in) tall
13 *Pennisetum orientale* × 3, 90cm (36in) tall
14 *Sedum* 'Herbstfreude', 60cm (24in) tall
15 *Pennisetum alopecuroides* 'Woodside', 80cm (32in) tall
16 *Miscanthus sinensis* 'Little Kitten', 30cm (12in) tall

Cortaderia selloana 'Pumi
Bright plumes are highly conspicuous when they first appear in late summ lasting until spring.

Stipa gigantea
Dark, evergreen leaves and tall wands of golden flowerheads.

Perovskia 'Blue Spire'
Wisps of fragrant, silvery leaves below spires of blue flowers.

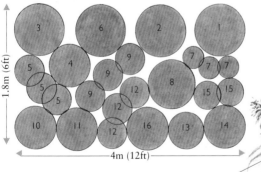

1.8m (6ft)

4m (12ft)

Miscanthus sinensis 'Ferner Osten' Flowers start out rich crimson then turn silver and finally buff. They last well through winter.

Liatris spicata Tufts of grassy leaves topped in mid- to late summer with bottlebrush-like spikes of intense violet, flowering from the top down.

Carex petriei Makes low tussocks of intensely foxy-red leaves, which are showy the whole year through.

SPRING FLOWERS

Anemone blanda
Bergenia 'Sunningdale'
Camassia quamash
Crocuses
Daffodils
Doronicum orientale
Fritillaria imperialis
Leucojum vernum
Snowdrops
Tulips

Eupatorium purpureum 'Gateway' Purple-pink flowerheads in late summer. Seedheads last into winter.

Calamagrostis × *acutiflora* 'Karl Foerster' The classic vertical-accent grass.

Panicum virgatum 'Blue Tower' Tall and powdery blue, with a buff skeleton in winter.

Phyllostachys aureosulcata 'Aureocaulis' Eye-catching bamboo with tall, bright canes. Draws the eye all year, especially in winter.

Lythrum virgatum 'Dropmore Purple' Spires of vibrant purple flowers from mid- to late summer.

Sedum 'Herbstfreude' Flat heads of pinkish flowers that turn dark red then brown, lasting all winter.

...dbeckia fulgida '...oldsturm' Bold yellow ...d brown daisy flowers ...at are good for picking.

Miscanthus sinensis 'Little Kitten' Ideal for the front of the border. Lasts well into winter.

Pennisetum orientale Early to flower, making pinkish-mauve flower spikes from early to late summer.

Pennisetum alopecuroides 'Woodside' Rich, pinkish-brown flowerheads in late summer.

SUMMER BEDDING

Annual grasses usually flower far more freely than perennial types, and they are best in drifts with contrasting flowerheads next to one another; sow seed on bare soil where they are to flower, in areas marked out with sand or spray paint. Remove any unusual seedlings or weeds as they develop in spring. Rudbeckias, cornflowers, cleomes, and foxgloves make good companions. This display is shown at its peak in late summer.

Coix lacryma-jobi Tall grass with huge, showy seeds, but needs long, hot summers to fruit freely.

Pennisetum villosum Grey-green clumps with shaggy flowerheads that are icy-green at first, then fading to buff.

Briza maxima Large, locket-shaped flowers borne in showy heads. It provides interest earlier than the other grasses in this group.

Lagurus ovatus Small, weedy tufts of slender, upright stems topped by fluffy, oval flowerheads like tiny rabbits' tails. It is quite different in form to the other grasses.

PLANTING PLAN

1 *Coix lacryma-jobi*, to 1.2m (4ft) tall
2 *Pennisetum setaceum* 'Rubrum', 60cm (24in) tall
3 *Avena sterilis*, 1m (3ft) tall
4 *Pennisetum villosum*, 60cm (24in) tall
5 *Hordeum jubatum*, 30cm (12in) tall
6 *Lagurus ovatus*, 30cm (12in) tall
7 *Briza maxima*, 30cm (12in) tall
8 *Lamarckia aurea*, to 30cm (12in) tall

1.8m (6ft)

3m (10ft)

Pennisetum setaceum 'Rubrum'
Rich, chocolate-brown leaves
and mahogany-crimson
bottlebrush flowers make
this tender perennial the
centrepiece of this scheme.

Avena sterilis Slender,
arching stems from
which hang flowers
shaped like wide-open
tweezers. Excellent for
picking and drying.

Hordeum jubatum
Large, barley-like
flowers of vibrant pink in
midsummer, often with a
second flush in autumn. Its
seedheads soon shatter.

Lamarckia aurea Unusual
grass with downward-
pointing flowers in silky
yellow flowerheads,
sometimes flushed
purple, in early summer.

LOOKING AFTER GRASSES

CHOOSING AND BUYING GRASSES

MOST GRASSES ARE EASY TO GROW and will establish quickly. Since a huge number of different types are available, however, varying in size and cultural requirements, it is important to make sure that the grasses you buy are suitable for your garden. Match large grasses to large places, sun-lovers to sunny places, and so on. If in doubt, check the label or ask for advice. Specialist nurseries will be able to help you with less common types.

WHAT TO LOOK FOR

Look for plants with springy, colourful foliage. If possible, tip the grass out of its pot and examine the roots, which should be well-spaced, vigorous, and pale in colour or white. There should be sufficient roots to bind the soil; if they have become congested, reject the plant as it may have been in its pot too long. In addition, always avoid grasses whose roots are thin, brown, and dense, because they will be difficult to establish. Plants with discoloured or dying leaves should also be avoided, except in autumn when many grasses die back naturally. Finally, do not buy a plant in soil that has been neglected and allowed to dry out, as it will subsequently be difficult to re-wet and establish.

Springy, colourful foliage shows no signs of drought or discoloration

HEALTHY PLANT
As well as vigorous top-growth, always check for a healthy and well-developed root system.

BUYING TIPS

• Look for vigorous plants with good foliage. There should be no evidence of very recent repotting.
• Dry, rolled-up leaves and pot-bound roots are a sign of neglect.
• Buy smaller plants rather than larger ones. Small plants usually grow on better at home.
• Make sure the plant is suitable for your site and soil. Read the label or ask for advice.
• Cheap plants might be of low quality.

ORANGE CANES Phyllostachys aureosulcata *'Aureocaulis' adds a strong vertical element.*

PREPARING THE GROUND

WHERE AN EXTENSIVE PLANTING OF GRASSES is intended, the simplest plan is to clear the ground with weedkiller well in advance of planting time. The ground should then be dug over, which will aerate it, and grit or sand worked into the soil to improve drainage and impoverish the soil. The ground should then be left to weather for about three months and only be broken down into a fine tilth at planting time.

CLEARING THE GROUND OF WEEDS

Ensure the ground is weed-free before planting. Either weed by hand (*see right*) or use a glyphosate weedkiller, which will destroy the roots of persistent weeds. Three applications are usually necessary.

WEEDKILLERS
• Some perennial weeds are very difficult to eradicate by hand. Combine forking with repeated applications of weedkiller.
• Weedkillers are effective, but they can be expensive. Ensure maximum success and safety by carefully following all instructions.

TACKLING WEEDS BY HAND AND FORK
Perennial weeds are best forked out in summer, because the warm weather helps by drying out and killing the exposed roots.

DIGGING OVER AND IMPOVERISHING THE SOIL

Most grasses are plants of poor soils, so rather than enriching the soil as for other plants, it is better to impoverish it. This can be done by forking in quantities of gravel or pea grit. In the case of most sedges and a few grasses, the plants prefer damper soils. To improve the moisture-holding capacity of a soil, simply add plenty of organic matter, such as spent hops or garden compost, in place of the pea grit or gravel.

1 **Add a generous amount of pea grit** to an area of soil that has been previously dug over. Avoid cultivating the soil when it is wet or frozen, or you may damage its structure.

2 **Fork the pea grit** into the soil, thoroughly mixing it in as you proceed. Work backwards so you do not compact the earth that you have just turned over.

PLANTING GRASSES

Ideally, grasses should be planted in either spring or autumn when the ground is warm but winter will do so long as the ground is not frozen or waterlogged. Before planting, water grasses well; place the potted grass into a bucket of water until the bubbles stop, then remove and let it drain. Prepare a planting hole four times as large as the pot. Tip plant out of pot and plant slightly deeper than it was in the pot. Water well.

1 **Check the planting hole** is a similar depth to the root ball of the plant. Remove or add more soil from the hole as necessary.

2 **Turn the plant** upside down and carefully remove the container. Gently tease out the roots to help them to grow into the soil.

3 **Return the soil** to the planting hole and firm around the roots with the toe or heel of your foot. Water the plant in thoroughly.

PLANTING TIPS

• Water grasses in well after planting. After that they should need little further watering. Too much water makes the growth floppy and prone to disease.

• Watch for rolled leaves. This shows grasses need watering. Their leaves are normally flat.

PLANTING DISTANCES
Space plants half their ultimate height apart in a border. Closer planting may cause crowding; wider gaps will leave opportunities for weeds.

PLANTING IN CONTAINERS

Most grasses look superb in pots. Make sure there is a drainage hole or holes in the bottom. Cover the bottom with small stones or crocks from broken pots to aid drainage. Partially fill the container with soil-based compost (peat-based composts dry out too quickly). Position the plant allowing space for watering, then back fill with more compost and water well. Finally mulch with gravel, bark or beads. Give bamboos in containers plenty of space, and never let them dry out.

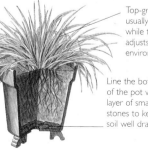

Top-growth usually pauses while the plant adjusts to its environment

Line the bottom of the pot with a layer of small stones to keep the soil well drained

PLANTING & CONTROLLING BAMBOOS

BAMBOOS WILL ONLY DO AS WELL as the planting hole you prepare for them, and they are greedy feeders. Prepare a hole 60–90cm (24–36in) wide and 30–45cm (12–18in) deep and mix in well-rotted farmyard manure, garden compost, or a slow-release fertilizer. Soak the bamboo in a bucket before planting, and plant a little deeper than it was in the pot. Water in well.

DIFFERENT ROOT SYSTEMS

Bamboos are either clumpers or runners, depending on their type of root system. Clumping bamboos, such as yellow-groove bamboo (*Phyllostachys aureosulcata*), have compact root systems and tend to stay where they are planted. Running bamboos, such as *Sasa* and *Pleioblastus*, have roots that spread in all directions and are capable of taking over large areas. Nurserymen can tell you which type is which.

USEFUL TIPS
• Plant bamboos in good light, but out of full sun.
• For optimum growth, mulch and fertilize around the roots in spring.
• Choose a sheltered site.
• Never let the roots dry out. Install a weeping hose if necessary.

RUNNING RHIZOMES
The tips of the rhizomes grow horizontally underground, and new canes spring up behind.

CLUMPING BAMBOO
The rhizomes do not run; instead the tips turn up and develop into new canes.

CONTROLLING SPREAD

The invasive spread of some bamboos can be controlled either by burying a flexible plastic barrier around the plant, obtainable from specialist bamboo nurseries, or by confining in containers. Alternatively, a circular section of a large-diameter drainage pipe can be used to surround the bamboo. Many gardeners find that it is easier to chop out rhizomes with a spade (*see opposite*).

BARRIERS & CONTAINERS

• Flexible plastic barriers need to be installed vertically, with 8–10cm (3–4in) above the ground, and the joints bolted together to prevent the rhizomes from slipping through.
• Large-diameter, concrete drainage pipes are the type used to drain water from motorways. They are circular in cross-section, 1–1.2m (3–4ft) in diameter. However, they can be rather expensive, heavy, and difficult to install.

CONTROLLING RHIZOMES MANUALLY

The rhizomes of most running varieties can be controlled quite easily with a spade. The rhizomes of most running bamboos are relatively soft and easy to cut through when they are young. The procedure is to dig a trench about 30cm (12in) wide and deep all round the clump that you want to contain. You then fill this trench with some light, soft material that is easy to dig through, such as lawn mowings, garden compost, or seaweed. The rhizomes will grow horizontally into this soft material where they are easy to reach and to sever. Remove the severed sections; they will harden if left, which will make it difficult to thrust the spade into the trench in future years.

1 **Sharpen the tip** of the spade using a sharpening stone. This will help the spade chop through the rhizomes, which are often quite tough.

2 **Dig a trench** about 30cm (12in) deep around the perimeter of the bamboo to expose the rhizomes. Mound up the soil around the trench.

3 **Chop through** the spreading rhizomes where they emerge from the inside wall of the trench. Resharpen the spade as necessary.

4 **Follow the cut rhizome** into the soil outside the perimeter of the trench using a fork. Lift out and dispose of the unwanted rhizome.

5 **Scrape the soil** back into the trench. Alternatively, the trench can be refilled with soft material, making the job easier next season (*see top*).

USEFUL TIPS

• Reserve a special spade for chopping off rhizomes. Keep the cutting edge sharp with a sharpening stone.

• Make life easy – grow a bamboo that doesn't run, such as *Chusquea couleou*, *Fargesia murieliae*, *F. nitida*, and *Thamnocalamus*.

• Invasive bamboos include species of *Chimonobambusa*, *Phyllostachys*, *Pleioblastus*, *Sasaella*, and *Sasa*.

• If bamboos get out of control, cut them down and spray the regrowth with a glyphosate weedkiller. It may take several doses.

ESTABLISHMENT AND AFTERCARE

G RASSES NEED LITTLE ROUTINE MAINTENANCE once planted, provided that weeds have been thoroughly cleared from the ground before planting (*see p.48*). One technique gardeners might find extremely useful is to spread a layer of mulch onto the surface of the soil after planting, which will repress weeds, keep the soil moist, and generally improve the growing environment. Annual grooming in winter or early spring will keep ornamental grasses at their finest.

FEEDING, WATERING, AND MULCHING

Most grasses are plants of poor soils and will become floppy and prone to disease if you feed them. Exceptions are large grasses, such as pampas grass (*Cortaderia selloana*) and eulalia grasses (*Miscanthus*), which need occasional feeding to maintain their vigour. Use well-rotted farmyard manure or slow-release fertilizer, such as bone meal.

Only water grasses when you plant them, and during their first season if they they roll their leaves, which is a sign of distress. Grasses are the most efficient of all plants at extracting and using water, and they seldom need watering once established. During long, hot summers, however, it is wise to check for signs of drought.

ROLLED-UP LEAF
Grass leaves roll up in times of drought or water stress to conserve moisture. Act immediately by watering well.

HEALTHY LEAF
Flat and brightly coloured leaf blades are a sign that the grass is well, but continue to check for signs of stress.

APPLYING MULCH
Pea-grit or gravel suits grasses best (here, Carex oshimensis 'Evergold'), and organic materials like shredded bark are most attractive around sedges, rushes, and bamboos. Apply them when the soil is moist, but not too thickly, as the roots may become too wet and the plants will die.

MULCHING TIPS

• Weed-suppressing sheets or mats serve the same function as mulches, but these mats and sheets often look unattractive if left bare. Cover them with a thin layer of mulch to improve their appearance.

• Shingle, gravel, shredded bark, slate chippings, and glass beads are popular, readily available, and long-lasting mulches for ornamental grasses.

• Do not mulch heavily as the ground will then remain in a condition that is too wet for the roots of grasses, leading to floppy growth and poor resistance to pests and disease.

• Mulch bamboos with their own fallen leaves and chopped up canes to ensure that the soil has an even supply of silica. This is a mineral that the plants need to grow.

CUTTING BACK GRASSES

The only routine maintenance needed to keep grasses growing well, apart from weeding and the removal of broken flower stems, is an annual grooming. Grasses that turn biscuit-coloured in winter should be cut down nearly to ground level in late winter, and any debris left in the centre of the clump should be raked out using a spring-tined rake. Evergreen grasses and sedges and rushes simply need a light trim over – also in late winter – to remove the split ends of the leaves and old flower stems. When spring comes, fresh growth will replenish the display. In "natural" gardens, the material removed can be chopped finely and used as a mulch.

1 **Wait until** late winter before cutting back, once the display begins to look untidy. If left, new growth will be impeded.

2 **Cut back** all old stems close to ground level, using a pair of secateurs or shears, which are adequate tools for trimming most grasses.

3 **Rake out** debris from the centre of the clump with a spring-tined rake. Remove the material or chop it finely and spread it as a mulch.

USING LOPPERS
A pair of loppers or a saw may be necessary for grasses with thick stems or canes, like the eulalia grasses (Miscanthus).

USING A HEDGE TRIMMER
A powered hedge trimmer will make light work of cutting back grasses if you have many to trim back.

USEFUL TIPS

• When dealing with pampas grasses, wear tough leather gloves and protective eyewear. The edges of the leaves have vicious teeth.

• You can burn the dead leaves in the middle of your pampas grass instead of cutting them, but do this every year to get a quick, light fire. A fire made up of many years' leaves will be hot and may kill the clump.

• Some grasses, especially annuals, self-seed too freely. Cut back their heads as soon as flowering is over, before they turn to seed.

ROOTING OUT DEAD AND BROKEN CANES

Dead and broken canes can mar the strong, vertical characteristic of bamboos, but they are easily removed. Take out dead canes on an annual basis, and broken canes should be removed as soon as they are noticed. In both cases the canes should be cut off as close to the ground as possible using a pair of loppers. Canes that lean can also spoil a display, and the remedy is to remove some of leaves from the top of the cane.

REMOVAL OF A BROKEN CANE
Damaged canes will not regrow and must be removed completely at the base. Canes look odd and are dangerous if cut half way up.

THINNING OUT A DEAD CANE
The presence of dead canes will make a clump of bamboo look tired and old. Once removed, they have many uses around the garden.

CUTTING AND DRYING FLOWERHEADS

The flowerheads of most grasses suit indoor dried flower arrangements, and many grasses dry out naturally in the garden. If cut when too mature, however, they will shatter as soon as they come into the warmth of a house. It is usually better to pick the flowerheads just as the flowers are turning into seeds. Tie bunches of flower stems together with string, and hang them upside down in a drafty shed or airing cupboard. To retain the natural curve of the stems, dry the grasses upright in a vase.

DRIED FLOWERHEADS
Setaria italica *(left) and* Phalaris canariensis *(right) are two of the many grasses with attractive flowerheads suitable for drying.*

MORE TIPS
• Tie flowerheads together in several small bunches rather than a single large one. Small bunches will dry better and are less likely to tangle.
• Keep dried grasses out of direct sunlight, which will cause them to fade.
• Coat dried grasses with hairspray – it helps to make them longer-lasting.

SEASONAL HEADING

WINTER
- Cut out flower stems that have broken in wind, rain, or snow.
- Rake up leaves and debris from stem sheaths as they tend to blow around the garden.

CLEARING DEBRIS
Groom your grasses in late winter, removing dead foliage that will impede new growth.

- Comb catalogues for new, improved varieties, and for suggestions of better plant combinations.
- Plan new displays on squared paper to keep a sense of scale.
- Sow seeds of some annuals under glass for a longer growing season, such as *Coix lacryma-jobi, Hordeum jubatum, Panicum miliaceum, Sorghum nigrum,* and *Zea mays.*
- Propagate cool-season grasses – those that flower before midsummer (*see p.11*).
- Apply flowers of sulphur around grasses prone to rust.

SPRING
- Cut back deciduous grasses and rake out dead foliage (*see p.53*).
- Trim split ends of evergreen grasses.
- Weed and tidy.
- Start planting out new grasses.

- Pot on grasses that have outgrown their containers, and replace the soil around plants that have been in their pots for more than two or three years.
- Divide warm-season grasses – those that flower after midsummer (*see p.11*).
- Sow seed of perennial grasses and keep in a cool, shaded place until germinated. Prick the seedlings into single pots once they have two leaves (*see p.57*).
- Sow seed of annual grasses outside where they are to flower (*see p.44*).

SUMMER
- Thin young annual grasses to the required density.
- Water grasses in pots regularly, and watch for signs of water stress in newly planted grasses.
- Weed as necessary.
- Start to gather flowerheads of grasses to be dried for indoor display.
- Remove annuals that have finished flowering before they scatter their seed – unless self-seeding is wanted.
- Start to collect seed of grasses you may want to increase. Seed of many grasses can be sown as soon as it is ripe.
- Control running grasses by cutting through the runners with a sharp spade and pulling out the unwanted growth.
- Confine bamboos by chopping out rhizomes (*see p.51*).

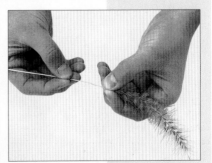

COLLECTING SEED
Seed should be collected as soon as it is ripe in summer or autumn. Store it in paper, not plastic, envelopes in a cool, dry place.

AUTUMN
- Gather flowerheads for indoor decoration before they deteriorate too far.
- Tidy wind-damaged grasses.
- Cut down and tidy the foliage of associated herbaceous plants that have died back.
- Collect and store seeds of grasses for next year.
- Start clearing the ground for new plantings to be made in spring.
- Plant spring-flowering bulbs, such as daffodils and tulips, among grasses in late winter and early spring. This will extend the season of interest
- Remove any annual grasses that have finished their display.

PROPAGATING GRASSES

GRASSES, INCLUDING SEDGES AND RUSHES, can all be increased either by division of clumps or by seed. Division is a very simple process that is especially handy for named cultivars, as these will not "come true" from seed. It is also useful where older clumps have died out in the middle and may be losing their vigour. Seed of spring-flowering grasses will produce new plants by autumn, and seed of later-flowering species sown in early winter will give new plants in spring.

DIVIDING SMALL CLUMPS

Grasses can be said to belong to one of two groups: warm-season grasses that flower after midsummer, and cool-season grasses that flower before midsummer. Divide warm-season types in spring only, and cool-season grasses in either spring or autumn.

Small grasses, such as fescues, can easily be divided by tearing the clumps apart by hand. Larger grasses, such as ribbon grass, may need to be torn apart with two large forks set back-to-back; if necessary, cut back the foliage for easier handling.

3 **Split the clump** into small sections. Trim the foliage and overlong or damaged roots from each division.

1 **Water the plant** well, here *Carex oshimensis* 'Evergold', then lift it from the soil with a fork. Shake off any loose soil.

4 **Replant each division** in a fresh pot or nursery bed, in sandy potting compost. Label and water well.

2 **Work your fingers** and thumbs into the root ball, then carefully begin to tear the clump apart.

PLANTS TO TRY

SMALLER GRASSES
Arrhenatherum
Briza
Carex
Deschampsia
Elymus
Festuca
Hakonechloa
Helictotrichon
Holcus
Imperata
Luzula
Melica
Milium
Stipa
Uncinia

LARGER GRASSES
Arundo
Calamagrostis
Cortaderia
Fargesia
Miscanthus
Molinia
Panicum
Pennisetum
Phalaris
Phyllostachys
Pleioblastus

Dealing with Large Plants

Large specimens like eulalia and pampas grasses have tough rootstocks and need forceful measures to divide them. Young plants can be split using a sharp spade, but mature clumps require an axe or bow-saw. Remove the top-growth first so you can get to the plant easily. The centre of the clump is discarded as it is less vigorous than the edges.

1 Dig up a clump (here, *Miscanthus sinensis* 'China') using a sharp spade. It will be heavy, so lift it carefully.

2 Split the clump with a bow-saw or axe. Wear gloves to protect your hands from any sharp stubs.

USING A LONG-HANDLED AXE *Stand with your legs apart when swinging an axe; if it misses, it will not hit a leg.*

Growing Plants from Seed

Best results always come from seed that is freshly collected and sown straight away, so remember to collect seed as soon as it is ripe. Run your finger and thumb together up the seedhead to gather seed, then sow in pots of seed compost (*see below*). Keep your seedlings growing well as they never recover from set backs. Seedlings sprouted in spring will be well-developed by autumn, and seed sown in early winter will yield new plants for spring. Seed can be stored over winter in a cool, dry place.

1 Scatter small seeds directly onto the surface of fine seed compost. Large seeds should be placed individually.

2 Cover with a thin layer of fine sand or more seed compost. A thin layer of pea grit will deter mice.

3 Allow seeds to germinate, and thin out as necessary. Transplant to individual pots when large enough to handle.

GRASS & BAMBOO GALLERY

THIS ALPHABETICAL CATALOGUE shows the tremendous range and diversity of ornamental grasses, bamboos, sedges, and rushes on offer. The majority are undemanding given a well-drained, sunny site, and most are fully hardy – needing no protection from frost. Specific cultivation details and descriptions are given for each plant, and design tips are supplied where a grass or bamboo is particularly suited to a certain use or position in the garden.

◎ *Prefers full sun* ◙ *Prefers light or dappled shade* ◪ *Prefers partial shade* ▣ *Tolerates full shade* ◊ *Prefers well-drained soil* ◔ *Prefers moist soil* ◕ *Prefers wet soil* ✱ *Half hardy (down to 0°C/23°F)* ✱✱ *Frost hardy (down to -5°C/23°F)* ✱✱✱ *Fully hardy (down to -15°C/5°F)* ❁ *Frost tender* ♡ *RHS Award of Garden Merit*

A

Agrostis nebulosa
(Cloud bent grass)
This annual grass produces huge, diffuse flowerheads in summer that look like billowing clouds of pale buff above the ridiculously small leaves. Sow seed in spring or autumn where the plants are to flower.
◎◊ ✱✱✱
↕↔ 30cm (12in)

Alopecurus pratensis 'Aureovariegatus'
(Golden foxtail grass)
Among the brightest of yellow-variegated grasses, golden foxtail grass has narrow leaves that are mostly borne horizontally, and they are either green with vivid yellow margins and stripes, or

ALOPECURUS PRATENSIS 'AUREOVARIEGATUS'

wholly yellow. The flowers are produced in early summer, but are best removed; if left, the plants go into summer dormancy. Best in sun and needs frequent division on heavy soils to maintain vigour.
◎◊ ✱✱✱
↕ 1.2m (4ft) ↔ 40cm (16in)

Andropogon gerardii
(Big bluestem)
An upright, strictly clump-forming, perennial grass with an abundance of blue-green leaves and stems. These take on orange, red, and wine-red colours in autumn, fading to buff or beige in winter. The reddish brown flowers look like chickens' feet. Needs poor, well-drained soil.
◎◊ ✱✱✱
↕ 2m (6ft) ↔ 60cm (24in)

Arrhenatherum elatius subsp. *bulbosum* 'Variegatum'
(Striped bulbous couch grass, Onion grass)
A cool-season grass that is at its best in late spring and early summer, becoming semi-dormant later. It forms dense mounds of narrow, spreading foliage; the leaves are

HAPPY COUPLE *Tall* Spartina pectinata *and short* Hakonechloa macra *meet along a garden path.*

margined and striped bright white – one of the showiest of all white-variegated grasses. It grows best in shade, which will not diminish the intensity of the variegation. Prone to foliar rust infections when grown in sun. Frequent division is necessary to maintain vigour.
◩ – ▦♀◊ ✿✿✿
‡↔ 30cm (12in)

Arundo donax
(Giant reed, Provencal reed)
This is the largest frost-hardy, perennial grass. It forms large to very large clumps of thick, stiffly upright blue-grey stems with very broad, blue-grey leaves symmetrically spaced in two ranks. It seldom flowers in cold climates, and the top-growth normally dies back to ground level in winter. Variety *versicolor* (syn. 'Variegata') is only half hardy, but it has the most dramatically variegated foliage of any grass, with grey-green leaves broadly striped rich cream – lovely in a conservatory or for a summer bedding display.
◩◊ ✿✿✿
‡4.2m (13ft) ↔ 1.5m (5ft)

BRIZA MAXIMA

BOUTELOUA GRACILIS

B

Bouteloua gracilis (syn. *Chondrosum gracile*)
(Blue grama grass, Mosquito grass)
Called mosquito grass because of the curious way the flowers hang down below the flower stems, supposedly like the larvae of mosquitos hanging from the surface of water, this grass forms low clumps of thin, dark green leaves. The flowering part of the stem is at right angles to the main stem. It needs a hot, dry site.
◩◊ ✿✿✿
‡60cm (24in) ↔ 30cm (12in)

Briza maxima
(Greater quaking grass)
An annual grass that forms dense clumps of foliage. Above these, from late spring to late summer, locket-shaped spikelets dangle on thin stems and dance in the wind. It self-seeds freely. *B. media* is taller and perennial, with smaller spikelets, and *B. minor* is a shorter and very dainty annual.
◩◊ ✿✿✿
‡30cm (12in) ↔ 25cm (10in)

C

Calamagrostis × acutiflora 'Karl Foerster'
(Feather reed grass)
This perennial grass is grown for its early flowers. It is useful as a vertical accent in border schemes, moving gracefully in the wind. It forms tight clumps or tussocks of thin, mid-green leaves, above which form thin stems of purple-tinted, feathery flower-heads in early summer. These mature to foxy-red seedheads and remain attractive into winter; it does not self-seed. The growth becomes floppy in rich soils and shade. 'Overdam' is smaller, with leaves edged and striped white.
◩ – ◩◊ ✿✿✿
‡1.8m (6ft) ↔ 60cm (24in)

Calamagrostis brachytricha (syn. *Acnatherum brachytricha, Stipa brachytricha*)
(Korean feather reed grass)
A perennial grass with large, late summer, oval flowerheads richly pink- and purple-tinted at first, fading to off-white

CALAMAGROTIS × ACUTIFLORA 'KARL FOERSTER'

CAREX (SEDGES)

Sedges are distinguished by their triangular leaves and stems. Generally, they are low-growing and do best in damper soil or more shady sites than true grasses. All are perennial and evergreen unless stated otherwise.

C. berggrenii forms stubby, dense tufts to 10cm (4in) tall of brown to silvery-brown foliage. The summer flowers are almost black.

C. buchananii (Leatherleaf sedge, red fox sedge) has rolled leaves with pig-tail-like curls at the tips. It grows on well-drained soil and withstands drought when established. To 75cm (30in).

C. comans is best revealed in a tall pot, with the foliage hanging vertically down. It reaches 60cm (24in). The bronze form and the similar *C. flagillifera*, 'Small Red', and 'Frosted Curls' all have coloured foliage.

C. conica 'Snowline' forms neat, dense tufts to 15cm (6in) tall of white-edged, dark green leaves.

C. elata 'Aurea' ♀ (Bowles' golden sedge) in spring is outstandingly colourful, forming mounds to 70cm (28in) tall of arching yellow leaves with random dark green stripes.

C. morrowii 'Variegata' forms clumps of white-margined leaves to 60cm (24in) tall. 'Fisher's Form' has cream margins.

C. muskingumensis (Palm leaf sedge) bears narrow, greenish yellow foliage and small brown flowers in early summer. To 60cm (24in) tall. For wet or moist soil. 'Oehme' has gold-edged leaves.

C. oshimensis 'Evergold' ♀ forms dense tussocks to 30cm (12in) tall of arching, glossy creamy green leaves with dark green margins. *C. ornithopoda* 'Variegata' resembles a dwarf form.

C. pendula (Pendulous or weeping sedge) is one of the largest sedges, to 2m (6ft) tall in flower, with pendent green catkin-like flowerheads at the tips of slender, arching stems. The leaves are bold and deep green. It may self-seed too freely; 'Moonraker' is smaller with creamy new leaves produced through summer in cool climates. It comes almost true from seed.

CAREX PENDULA

C. riparia 'Variegata' (Striped greater pond sedge) is dramatic in early spring when new white leaves emerge amid the black flowerheads. The leaves become margined then wholly green. Grow in water or very wet ground. It can be invasive, especially if it reverts to the green form.

C. siderosticha 'Variegata' (Broad-leaved sedge) is a short, deciduous woodland sedge to 30cm (12in) tall with white-striped leaves.

C. 'Silver Sceptre' grows to 30cm (12in) tall with arching leaves, which may scorch in sun and burn in frost.

C. testacea, to 1.5m (5ft) tall, has curious yellow leaves, turning orange in sun, green in shade. *C. dipsacea* is similar.

C. trifida forms big clumps of broad leaves. The flowers appear in stubby spikes, only just showing above the leaves.

CAREX ELATA 'AUREA' ♀

then buff. The seedheads remain intact through winter. A tidy grass, usually upright-divergent in habit, sometimes arching or loosely clustered.

◎ – ▨◊ – ◊ ❅ ❅ ❅
↕ 1.2m (4ft) ↔ 60cm (24in)

Chasmanthium latifolium (syn. Uniola latifolia)
(Sea oats, Spangle grass)
A clump-forming perennial grass from rich, moist North American woodlands. It is treasured for its stiffly dangling flowers, which look like little lockets made of mahogany. They are borne in late summer on the arching tips of thread-thin stems. It needs sun in cool climates.

◎ – ▨◊ ❅ ❅ ❅
↕ 1m (3ft) ↔ 60cm (24in)

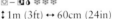
CHIONOCHLOA CONSPICUA

Chimonobambusa marmorea
(Marbled bamboo)
The bunched branches and leaves of this very distinctive bamboo, give it a lush appearance. The canes are thick-walled and have prominent nodes. Its common name derives from the new cane sheaths, which are marbled. When growing well, it can become very invasive; the canes are usually 2m (6ft) tall, but may reach 3m (10ft) in warm climates.

▨◊ ❅ ❅ ❅
↕ 2–3m (6–10ft) ↔ indefinite

Chionochloa conspicua
(Hunangamoho, Plumed tussock grass)
Forming rounded, evergreen tussocks, this perennial grass bears huge, feathery and drooping, one-sided flowerheads in summer. These flowerheads are similar to those of pampas grasses (*Cortaderia*), but they are

CORTADERIA (PAMPAS GRASS)

These large and spectacular perennial grasses form huge tussocks of sharp-edged, evergreen leaves. White- or pink-shaded, silky plumes tower above the foliage. They need to be grown in well-drained soil in full sun.

CORTADERIA SELLOANA
'AUREOLINEATA' ♀

C. richardii (New Zealand pampas grass, Toe toe) flowers in early summer, forming silvery white, shaggy flowerheads to 2.5m (9ft) tall, which last into winter.

C. selloana flowers in late summer or autumn. Some of the best cultivars are: 'Albolineata' (syn. 'Silver Stripe'), to 1.2m (4ft) tall, has white-striped leaves. 'Aureolineata' ♀ (syn. 'Gold Band') has leaves striped rich yellow. 'Pink Feather' has pink-tinted flowers. 'Pumila' ♀, dwarf pampas grass, with creamy white flowers, reaches 1.5m (5ft) tall. 'Rendatleri', pink pampas grass, has loose, rich pink plumes, but the stems often break in exposed sites. 'Silver

CORTADERIA SELLOANA
'SUNNINGDALE SILVER' ♀

Comet' has white-striped leaves; 'Silver Fountain' is similar to the foregoing but more robust; 'Sunningdale Silver' ♀ is a outstanding clone with huge, weather-resistant white plumes.

cream rather than white. Most chionochloas are outstandingly beautiful grasses, but mostly rather tricky in cultivation. Other recommended species include: *C. flavescens* and *C. flavicans*, with much looser, greenish yellow plumes in spring and summer respectively (the latter must have strong sun and cool nights to flower), and *C. rubra*, which is grown for its bright coppery red winter foliage that is less intense in summer.

◫ – ▨◊ ❋❋
‡2m (6ft) ↔ 1m (3ft)

Chusquea culeou ♥
(Chilean bamboo, Foxtail bamboo)
A tall bamboo with thick, solid canes that are often upright but usually arch under the weight of the foliage. The canes produce many fine branches, ending in an abundance of small leaves. Newly emerging canes are covered in pale, suede-like sheaths, which soon fall. Once seen, it is never confused with other bamboos. It is hardy and wind-resistant in coastal

COIX LACRYMA-JOBI

CHUSQUEA CULEOU

areas, but it is less happy in hot, dry gardens.

◫ – ▨◊ ❋❋❋
‡6m (20ft) ↔ 2.5m (8ft)

Coix lacryma-jobi
(Christ's tears, Job's tears)
A tufted, tropical annual grass cultivated since biblical times for its huge, showy grains, which have been used for beads or even money. It can be grown in a summer border, but it needs very long, hot summers to fruit freely.
In cold climates, the seeds must be sown in a heated greenhouse in midwinter, and the young plants potted on to keep them growing well. They should be hardened off once the frosts are over and set out in their final positions in summer.

◫◊ ❋
‡1.2m (4ft) ↔ 2.5m (8ft)

Cyperus longus
(Galingale)
This perennial sedge forms running clumps of upright stems, with shiny green leaves produced in whorls at the tips, like the spokes of a wheel. The flowers are reddish brown, borne in

clusters above the foliage in summer. A plant for shallow water, 15–30cm (6–12in) deep, or damp ground.

◫ – ▨◊ – ◊ ❋❋❋
‡45–100cm (18–39in)
↔ 1m (3ft) or more

D

Deschampsia cespitosa
(Tufted hair grass, Tussock grass)
This tightly tufted, clump-forming, evergreen perennial grass flowers in early to midsummer, producing ethereal, cloud-like flowerheads composed of tiny flowers at the tips of thread-like stems. It is best in damp soils and tolerates shade. There are many cultivars available that differ in flower colour and stature: 'Bronzeschleier' (syn. Bronze Veil) grows to 90cm (36in) tall and is a popular selection with shimmering bronze flowers, although the leaves are prone to infection by rust; 'Goldgehänge' (syn. Golden Pendant, Golden Shower)

DESCHAMPSIA CESPITOSA
'GOLDTAU'

has golden yellow flowers on pendent stems; 'Goldschleier' (syn. Golden Veil) has greenish yellow flowers; 'Goldtau' (syn. Golden Dew') grows to 90cm (36in) tall with more open, yellowish green flowerheads; 'Northern Lights' forms small tufts but still has tall flowering stems to 75cm (30in) above leaves that are dramatically margined and striped cream and flushed pink when new growth first appears in cool climates.
◎ – ◙◊ – ◊ ❋ ❋ ❋
‡ 1.2–2m (4–6ft)
↔ 1.2–1.5m (4–5ft)

Deschampsia flexuosa
(Wavy hair grass)
Similar in appearance to *D. cespitosa*, but smaller in all its parts, the leaves create a very fine texture, and the tiny flowers vary in colour from bronze to yellowish green. It will grow in dry shade. 'Tatra Gold' has gaudy, yellowish green foliage, especially in early summer, and showy, red-brown flowers.
◎ – ◙◊ – ◊ ❋ ❋ ❋
‡ 60cm (24in) ↔ 30cm (12in)

Deschampsia cespitosa 'Tatra Gold'

Elymus hispidus

E

Elymus hispidus (syn. *E. glaucus of gardens*)
(Blue wheatgrass, Hairy couch, Intermediate wheatgrass)
An eye-catching, perennial grass with intensely electric blue leaves, which grow to about 20cm (8in) long; at first, they are upright, later more spreading, and fade to beige in winter. The early to midsummer flowers appear in wheat-like spikes, the same intense blue as the leaves and stems, ripening to the colour of straw. *E. magellanicus* is similar but is shorter with a loose, floppy habit, and it is not reliably perennial.
◎◊ ❋ ❋ ❋
‡ 75cm (30in) ↔ 40cm (16in)

Eragrostis curvula
(African love grass)
This enchanting perennial with narrow and arching, evergreen leaves creates fine-textured clumps. In summer, thin, arching stems bear tiny, nodding spikelets creating a haze of grey above the leaf

mound. It self-seeds too freely in some soils. Useful as ground cover.
◎◊ ❋ ❋
‡↔ 1.2m (4ft)

Eriophorum angustifolium
(Common cotton grass)
This showy relative of the sedges needs constantly wet ground. Through summer and autumn it produces what look like fluffy white balls of cotton wool at the tops of slender stems. The leaves are dark green, and it has a spreading, running rootstock. Ideal beside a wildlife pool or in a bog garden.
◎◊ ❋ ❋ ❋
‡ 45cm (18in) ↔ indefinite

F

Fargesia murieliae ♀ (syn. *F. spathacea of gardens*)
(Muriel's bamboo)
A most elegant bamboo forming graceful clumps of tall, arching canes, which can be planted as a hedge or screen. The canes are bright green at first, maturing to yellow, bearing usually five

Fargesia murieliae ♀

FESTUCA VALESIACA 'SILBERSEE'

GLYCERIA MAXIMA
VAR. *VARIEGATA*

thin branches at each node. An abundance of small, soft green leaves weighs down the tops of the canes, causing them to arch over. Dwarf cultivars include: 'Harewood', 1m (3ft) tall, 'Simba', 1.9m (6ft) tall, and 'Thyme', 1.5m (5ft) tall. 'Jumbo' is exceptionally tall, at 4m (12ft). *F. nitida* ♀ is of a similar height and appearance to *F. murieliae* but has more upright, purple canes, the new canes lack leaves until their second season, and the leaves are narrower. *F. nitida* 'Eisenach' has notably small leaves, while 'Nymphenburg' has a weeping habit. Both tend to lose their leaves in winter but soon put on fresh leaves in spring.
◐ – ◙◊ ✳ ✳ ✳
↕ 3.8m (11½ft) ↔ 1.5m (5ft)

Festuca glauca
(Blue fescue, Grey fescue)
A small perennial grass that forms dense, bun-shaped mounds. It is lovely planted with spring bulbs and is best on sharply drained soils. Divide clumps every two to three years to maintain

vigour. The leaves are very narrow, creating fine-textured, usually silvery blue clumps, varying from deep to bright greens through to khaki and yellow. The flowers and stems of early and midsummer are the same colour as the leaves but fade to beige or straw. Many varieties are available – some of the best are: 'Azurit', with foliage more blue than silvery; intensely silver-blue 'Blaufuchs' (syn. Blue Fox) ♀; silver-blue 'Elijah Blue' with blue-grey flowers reaching 40cm (16in) tall; short and luminous yellow 'Golden Toupee', to 20cm (8in) tall; 'Harz', a darker, heavier shade of blue than others; and the very fine green 'Seeigel' (syn. Sea Urchin). *F. valesiaca* is similar to *F. glauca*, with frosted flowers. *F. valesiaca* 'Silbersee' (syn. Silver Sea) is more silvery than blue. *F. punctoria*, hedgehog fescue, has rigid blue-green leaves that are rolled and curved like upturned claws. Each leaf ends in a sharp point. It is the epitome of aridity.
◙◊ ✳ ✳ ✳
↕ 30cm (12in) ↔ 25cm (10in)

FESTUCA GLAUCA
'BLAUFUCHS' ♀

G

Glyceria maxima var. *variegata* (syn. *G. aquatica variegata*)
(Striped or variegated manna grass)
A perennial, moisture-loving grass grown for its dramatic, creamy yellow-striped leaves, which are most conspicuous in spring when they are also tinted with pink. The intensity of the colouring fades as summer advances. It spreads persistently, especially in damp soils, in which it thrives. Also suitable for a large pond in water up to 15cm (6in) deep; grow in a basket to restrict spread.
◙◊ ✳ ✳ ✳
↕ 1.8m (6ft) ↔ indefinite

H

Hakonechloa macra
(Hakone grass)
A slowly spreading, perennial grass with a dense rootstock, forming mounds of cascading leaves, which take on wine-red hues in late summer and

HAKONECHLOA MACRA
'AUREOLA' ♀

autumn. The tiny flowers are produced on very thin, claret-red stems amid the foliage. All cultivars of this plant need moist, well-drained, humus-rich soils and some shade, and they all assume brilliant rust tones in winter. 'Alboaurea' ♀ grows to 30cm (12in) tall, and is popular for its rich golden yellow leaves with thin stripes of green, and red and white flecks. 'Aureola' is similar but lacks the flecked pattern, producing a brighter effect overall. Slightly taller 'Mediovariegata' has thin creamy white stripes down the centre of the green leaves.
◼◊ ✻✻✻
↕↔ 45cm (18in)

Helictotrichon sempervirens
(syn. *Avena candida*) ♀
(Blue oat grass)
The rounded mounds of intensely silvery blue, needle-like leaves of this grass are arranged symmetrically like a fibre-optic toy. Its flowers are borne on slender, arching stems, both the same colour as the leaves but ripening to rich straw yellow. Ants like to nest in the middle. Choose a

sunny site with sharp drainage. 'Pendula' has more strongly arched flower stems.
◻◊ ✻✻✻
↕ 1.2m (4ft) ↔ 60cm (24in)

× *Hibanobambusa tranquillans* 'Shiroshima'
A hybrid bamboo with strikingly variegated leaves that are richly striped creamy white and tinted pink or purple in sunlight. The foliage seldom shows any damage, even after severe winters. Its running root system needs moderate control.
◻ – ◼◊ – ◊ ✻✻✻
↕ 4m (12ft) ↔ indefinite

Holcus mollis
'Albovariegatus'
(Striped Yorkshire fog)
This shallowly creeping perennial grass has short and flat leaves striped blue-green and creamy white, which creates the overall effect of a whitish carpet. It is a cool-season grass, with pale green flowers in early summer, looking its best during spring and early summer, becoming semi-dormant thereafter. Dampish soil in partial shade is preferred. Deadhead to

HORDEUM JUBATUM

HOLCUS MOLLIS
'ALBOVARIEGATUS'

avoid self-seeding, as the offspring will be green-leaved and invasive.
◻ – ◼◊ ✻✻✻
↕ 20cm (8in) ↔ 45cm (18in)

Hordeum jubatum
(Foxtail barley, Squirrel tail grass)
One of the loveliest grasses, with showy and shimmering, barley-like, vibrant pink flower-heads in midsummer. The seed-heads soon shatter. Treated as an annual; it may become a weed if allowed to self-seed.
◻◊ ✻✻✻
↕ 45cm (18in) ↔ 30cm (12in)

Hystrix patula
(Bottlebrush grass)
A clump-forming grass, producing curious bottlebrush-like flowers, green at first, then white tinged with pink, finally tan. The foliage is thin and rather poor. It is one of the few grasses that will grow in dry shade; it also flourishes in well-cultivated conditions, but it may be damaged by strong sun. Good for picking, green or dry.
◻ – ◼◊ ✻✻✻
↕ 45cm (18in) ↔ 60cm (24in)

IMPERATA CYLINDRICA 'RUBRA'

I

Imperata cylindrica 'Rubra'
(syn. 'Red Baron')
(Japanese blood grass),
famed for its blood-red
foliage, this is a shallow-
rooted, slowly spreading,
perennial grass that produces
upright foliage. In spring, the
leaves are green and topped
with red, but they are wholly
blood-red by midsummer, the
colouring becoming more
saturated by autumn. The
colour of this plant is seen
to best advantage when
positioned with the sun
beyond it. It is best in moist,
fertile soil in sun, although it
tolerates some drought once
established.
◨ ◊ ❋ ❋
↕↔ 30cm (12in) or more

K

Koeleria glauca
(Blue hair grass)
A tufted perennial grass,
generally similar to blue
fescue (*Festuca glauca*),
but with somewhat broader
leaves, which are inrolled at
the edges, and much showier
flower spikes. Cream and
green flowers in dense,
upright spikes turn buff in
midsummer. It is showiest
when planted in drifts,
preferring alkaline soils.
◨ – ◨ ◊ ❋ ❋ ❋
↕ 20cm (8in) ↔ 30cm (12in)

LAGURUS OVATUS

L

Lagurus ovatus
(Hare's tail grass)
An annual grass producing an
abundance of dense, compact
green flowerheads. These fade
to creamy white. The seed
should be sown in spring
where plants are to flower.
'Nanus' is a dwarf form.
◨ ◊ ❋ ❋ ❋
↕↔ 30cm (12in)

JUNCUS (RUSHES)

Rushes are native to moist
or wet, sunny places and are
useful in or at the waterside
for their architectural
qualities. They make dense
bundles of very upright
or upright divergent stems.
Some forms are grown
for their corkscrew stems.

J. decipiens 'Curly-wurly'
(syn. 'Spiralis') has tightly
twisted stems, looking like a
ball of glossy green wire wool.
It self-seeds freely on damp,
acid soils. To 15cm (6in) tall.

J. effusus f. *spiralis*
(Corkscrew rush) looks
like a bundle of overgrown,
shiny, dark green corkscrews
sticking out of the ground. It
needs constant moisture and
grows to 30cm (12in) tall.

J. inflexus 'Afro' (Corkscrew
hard rush) also reaches 30cm
(12in) tall, but it differs
from the above species in
that the twisted stems are
grey-green and matt. It is
also compatible with most
average garden soils.

JUNCUS EFFUSUS 'SPIRALIS'

Leymus arenarius (syn.
Elymus arenarius)
(Blue lyme grass)
Probably the most intensely
blue of all hardy perennial
grasses, this grass is
unfortunately fast-spreading
on most soils, and vigorously
invasive on dry soils. It
is lovely where it can be
contained, such as in a large
container where it will need
copious feeding and watering.
The summer flowers are wheat-
like, the same colour as the
leaves, but ripening to buff.
◎◊ ✳✳✳
↕ 1m (3ft) ↔ indefinite

Luzula sylvatica
(syn. *L. maxima*)
(Common woodrush,
Greater woodrush)
This woodrush is the best
ground-cover grass for shaded
places, even dry ones. It forms
large tussocks of relatively
broad, evergreen leaves and
spreads slowly by surface
rhizomes, which root as they
spread. The brown flowers
are produced in flat heads
held well above the foliage. In
its native woodlands, it often
dries out during long, dry

LEYMUS ARENARIUS

summers and revives after
rainfall. Recommended
cultivars include: 'Aurea' with
golden yellow leaves, which
are especially bright in winter;
'Hohe Tatra', with green
leaves held oddly upright; the
leaves of 'Marginata' (syn.
'Aureomarginata') have thin
white margins; 'Taggart's
Cream' (syn. 'A. Rutherford'),
with white young foliage,
turning cream to green
through yellow.
◪◊ ✳✳✳
↕ 1m (3ft) ↔ indefinite

M

Melica altissima
'Atropurpurea'
(Melick grass, Siberian
melick)
Grown for its intensely
purple, one-sided flower
spikes in summer, which are
excellent for picking and
drying, this is a loosely
clump-forming perennial with
soft, hairy leaves and a
somewhat floppy habit. It is
best in sun, tolerating slight
shade only. *M. uniflora* is
shorter, to 60cm (24in) tall,
with brown-purple flower-

heads and tolerates full
shade and drier conditions;
'Variegata' has green leaves
with white central stripes
and purple bases.
◎ – ◪◊ ✳✳✳
↕ 90cm (36in)
↔ 40–80cm (16–32in)

Melinis repens (syn.
Rhynchelytrum repens)
(Natal grass)
A lovely annual grass
producing cloud-like heads
of tiny, fluffy, pinkish red
flowers in late summer. It
is showiest when grown in
bold drifts in association with
mauve Michaelmas daisies. In
cold climates, the seed should
be sown under glass in spring,
and the seedlings set out in a
warm, sunny, sheltered place
in early summer.
◎◊ ✳
↕ 30cm (12in)
↔ 60–100cm (14–39in)

Milium effusum 'Aureum'
(Bowles' golden grass,
Golden wood millet)
A short-lived, cool-season,
perennial grass that forms
small clumps of soft and limp,
golden yellow foliage. The

LUZULA SYLVATICA 'AUREA'

MELICA ALTISSIMA
'ATROPURPUREA'

MISCANTHUS (EULALIA GRASS)

A group of large, clump-forming perennial grasses – mostly 1.5–1.8m (5–6ft) tall – with fine foliage. They bear showy, many-fingered flower plumes above the leaves from midsummer. The leaves and seedheads assume pale buff or beige tones through winter. Best in moist but well-drained soil in sun.

M. sinensis ♀ (Eulalia grass, Japanese silver grass) has many variable cultivars. All are lovely, and the following are among the most distinct: 'China', to 1.5m (5ft) tall, is one of the earliest to flower, wine-red at first, fading silver then buff – variety *condensatus* 'Cabaret' and 'Cosmopolitan', and 'Ferne Osten' are similar. 'Flamingo' is early flowering and one of the best, with pinkish white plumes and narrow leaves. 'Gracillimus', maiden grass, forms mushrooming mounds of very narrow, dark green leaves that sway gracefully in

MISCANTHUS SINENSIS 'SILBERFEDER'

the wind, with silvery plumes in autumn. 'Graziella' has narrow leaves and abundant silvery flowers. 'Kleine Fontäne' has narrow leaves with thin-fingered, silvery plumes that arch upwards then weep. 'Kleine Silberspinne' is shorter, to 90cm (36in) tall, and has horizontally held, very narrow leaves and relatively large, silvery plumes. 'Malepartus' is outstanding with broad, white-striped leaves and stout stems to 2m (6ft) tall, bearing large, wine-red plumes in midsummer that turn silver then buff, the whole plant turning ochrous yellow in autumn – it is the standard by which the other cultivars are judged. 'Morning Light', striped or variegated maiden grass, is similar to 'Gracillimus' but the narrow leaves are edged white. Variety *purpurascens* is a thin-leaved cultivar to 1m (3ft) tall, with pale, ghostly plumes, and leaves that take on wine-red tints from midsummer – the colour intensifying as autumn approaches. 'Rotsilber' has broad leaves with conspicuous white midribs and stout stems bearing deep rich red plumes that turn silver then buff. 'Sarabande' is similar to 'Gracillimus' but with paler green, narrow leaves and showy silvery plumes freely produced and held well above the foliage. 'Silberfeder' is a tall form with silvery plumes to 2.4m (7½ft). 'Sirene' produces

MISCANTHUS SINENSIS 'ZEBRINUS'

large heads of silvery white flowers that fluff out when dry and move with every wind, above narrow leaves. 'Strictus' forms dense clumps of very upright stems with reddish plumes in autumn, and mid-green leaves transversely banded with old gold. 'Undine' is lightly built for a miscanthus, bearing narrow, bright green leaves and relatively large coppery pink plumes that soon fade to silver. 'Variegatus', striped eualia grass or variegated miscanthus, forms dramatic clumps of broad, brightly white-striped leaves with reddish plumes in autumn. 'Yakushima Dwarf' is exceptionally free-flowering with copper then silver plumes to 1m (3ft) tall above narrow leaves. 'Zebrinus', zebra grass, is loose and floppy and justly famed for its dark green, yellow-banded leaves and maroon plumes to 2.4m (7½ft) that fade to silver.

MOLINIA (MOOR GRASS)

These are densely tufted perennial grasses that perform best in damp or moisture-retentive soils. They are unique among ornamental grasses in being totally deciduous; the leaves and stems break away from the rootstock in winter rather than staying attached as with most other grasses. They are slow to establish, so it is best to buy larger plants rather than small ones. All flower from midsummer onwards.

MOLINIA CAERULEA SUBSP. ARUNINACEA

M. caerulea subsp. *arundinacea* (Tall moor grass) forms low, rounded mounds of narrow foliage, and the flowers begin to rise above this clump on slender stems in early summer, reaching up to 2.4m (7½ft) tall. Among the best cultivars are: 'Bergfreund', to 1.8m (6ft) tall, has tiny, foxy-brown flowers borne in huge, diffuse heads to create a cloud-like effect. 'Fontane',

to 1.5m (5ft) tall, bears heavy heads of dark grey flowers that weigh the tips of the stems down like a fountain. 'Karl Foerster' reaches 1.5m (5ft tall) with large heads of bronze flowers on upright or arching stems. 'Skyracer' is a North American cultivar with very tall, stiffly upright stems and narrow flowerheads to 2.4m (7½ft) – it is useful as a vertical accent set among shorter plants and the foliage turns clear gold in autumn. 'Transparent' reaches 1.8m (6ft) tall and produces tiny, dark flowers in diffuse, cloud-like heads, which cause the stems to arch gracefully. 'Windspeil' also measures 1.8m (6ft) tall when in full flower and bears its dense flowerheads on stems that are upright in dry weather but arch outwards like a fountain and almost touch the ground when wet – it does not perform well when small.

M. caerulea subsp. *caerulea* (Purple moor grass) and its cultivars are generally smaller than subsp. *arundinacea*, the foliage often assuming a lovely butter yellow in autumn. 'Edith Dudszus' grows to 90cm (36in) and is noted for its dark red-purple stems and almost black flowers on thin, divergent stems; 'Heidebraut' is the tallest at 1.5m (5ft) and also has the richest autumn foliage colour – the flowers are greyish with a hint of yellow, which makes them glisten in the sun; 'Moorhexe' has dark flowers and stems held close together and upright, up to 60cm (24in) tall; 'Strahlenquelle', to 90cm (36in) tall, has foxy-red flowers on divergent stems, which make the clump wider than high; 'Variegata' ♥, striped purple moor grass is dramatically striped cream in all its parts, the whole turning clear yellow in autumn.

MOLINIA CAERULEA 'WINDSPIEL'

MOLINIA CAERULEA SUBSP. *CAERULEA*

leaf colour is a subtle lemon-yellow in shade, and a garish orange-yellow in sun where, however, it soon becomes summer-dormant. It seeds itself lightly when well-suited to its environment. Naturally a woodlander, it will only tolerate full sun where soils are reliably moist.

◨ – ◨◊ ❁❁❁
‡↔ 30cm (12in)

P

Phalaris arundinacea
(Reed canary grass, Ribbon grass)
An aggressively spreading, perennial grass that is a troublesome weed in some parts of the world. As a result, it is usually grown in one of its less vigorous, variegated forms – variety *picta* – commonly known as gardeners' garters: 'Picta' ♀ is shorter, to 1.5m (5ft) tall with green leaves striped cream, never pink; 'Feesey' reaches 1.2m (4ft) tall with leaves much more brightly white-variegated and flushed pink in

*PHALARIS ARUNDINACEA
VAR. PICTA* ♀

PANICUM (PANIC GRASS)

Panicum virgatum (Switch grass) is a perennial prairie grass that varies greatly in stature and colour of the foliage and flowerheads. All forms flower in late summer to bear large, cloud-like heads of tiny flowers above the foliage mound. Grow in well-drained soil, in sun. 'Blue Tower' is one of the largest at 2.7m (9ft) tall, all parts of the plant being a soft, silvery blue. The foliage of 'Hänse Hermes' (90cm/36in tall) turns rich orange-red in autumn. 'Heavy Metal' is slow to establish and is stiffly upright to 90cm (36in), with blue-grey foliage and almost cream flowers in sparse heads. 'Prairie Sky', to 1.2m (4ft), has the best blue foliage, stems, and flowers but becomes floppy on rich soils. 'Rehbraun' is similar to 'Hänse Hermes' but taller. 'Rotstrahlbusch' is similar again but more upright. 'Rubrum', red-seeded switch grass, is the

PANICUM VIRGATUM 'HEAVY METAL'

name applied to any cultivar whose foliage is red-tinted in autumn. 'Shenandoah', at 1.2m (4ft) tall, assumes the richest red autumn colouring of the group. 'Squaw' has huge, diffuse, strongly pink-tinted flowerheads to 1.5m (5ft) tall, the leaves turning red and yellow in autumn – it becomes floppy in rich soils. 'Strictum' is stiff and narrowly upright to 1.2m (4ft), and the green leaves assume rich yellow autumn tones. 'Warrior', at 1.5m (5ft), produces huge heads of tiny purplish flowers and rich red foliage in autumn. P. 'Wood's Variegated' has striped leaves.

Panicum miliaceum 'Violaceum' (Purple hog millet) is a large annual to 90cm (36in) tall topped by many fingered, deep rich violet-purple, almost black flowerheads. Effective in drifts; start seed under glass for a long growing season.

PANICUM 'WOOD'S VARIEGATED'

PENNISETUM (FOUNTAIN GRASS)

Pennisetum alopecuroides (Fountain grass, Chinese fountain grass) is a variable perennial grass that typically forms rounded mounds of narrow, dark green leaves. A fountain effect is created by the densely packed, reddish brown flowerheads; these are like tiny foxes' tails and are borne in late summer at the tips of slender stems, which arch under their weight. The plant reaches an overall height of 90cm (36in) and prefers well-drained soil in sun. Popular cultivars include: 'Hameln', a dwarf at 45cm (18in) tall, and 'Woodside', taller at 75cm (30in) – both flower freely but the stems are stiffer and produce less of a fountain effect; 'Viridescens' is noted for its almost black flowers, but these are seldom produced in cool climates, unfortunately. All forms become bleached through summer to pale buff and the display lasts through winter. Effective in a mixed border.

PENNISETUM ALOPECUROIDES 'HAMELN'

P. macrourum (South African fountain grass) lacks the fountain-like habit of other species. It has stiffly upright stems and flowerheads, remarkable in its own right. The chaffy, almost white spikes of flowers, about the length and thickness of a pencil, catch and hold the light from the sky, which draws the eye strongly. It flowers in late summer and autumn, reaching up to 2m (6ft) in height. It is not fully hardy and may not survive cold winters; grow in well-drained soil in full sun.

P. orientale ♀ (Oriental fountain grass) has pale pink-mauve fluffy flower spikes, resembling bottle brushes, from early to late summer on slender stems above soft, grey-green leaves. It reaches 90cm (36in) tall and is one of the best grasses to grow with old roses and lavenders. It prefers well-drained soil in full sun.

P. setaceum ♀ (Tender fountain grass) is a tropical species that can be grown as an annual or overwintered under glass and used for bedding out or spot-planting in summer. Well-drained soil in sun is preferred. 'Rubra' is a popular form with purple or dark-chocolate leaves overtopped in late summer by dense, silky spikes of red-brown, hairy flowers. The plant reaches 60cm (24in) tall and can be increased by division in the greenhouse.

P. villosum (Ethiopian fountain grass) has the most fountain-like habit of the group, forming wide clumps. The shaggy flower spikes appear from early to late summer, ice-green at first, maturing to white, finally ripening to a bristly buff. The leaves are grey-green. It grows to 60cm (24in) tall and can be treated as an annual in cool-climate gardens, preferring well-drained soil in full sun.

PENNISETUM MACROURUM

PENNISETUM VILLOSUM

PHRAGMITES AUSTRALIS 'VARIEGATUS'

spring; 'Luteopicta', to 1.5m (5ft) tall, has bright yellow young leaves, becoming yellow-striped, and later dark green. All are best in moist soil, in sun.

◨ – ◙◊ – ◊ ✳✳✳
‡ 1.8m (6ft) ↔ indefinite

Phragmites australis (syn. P. australis)
(Common or Norfolk reed)
A huge, very invasive perennial reed of temperate wetlands. It is usually considered too aggressive for gardens, although 'Variegatus', with dramatically yellow-striped leaves, is very much less invasive and suitable for garden display, reaching 2.4m (7½ft) tall; it is best in moist, rather than wet, soil.

◨◊ – ◊ ✳✳✳
‡ 3m (10ft) ↔ indefinite

Phyllostachys aurea ♀
(Fishpole bamboo, Golden bamboo)
Named for its golden canes and yellow-green foliage when grown in strong sunlight, this tall bamboo is reliably compact in cool conditions. The canes are always rigidly upright and leafy, which makes it suitable for screens and hedges. The

lower nodes on mature canes are swollen. 'Holochrysa' has bright yellow canes.

◨ – ◙◊ ✳✳✳
‡ 8m (25ft) ↔ indefinite

Phyllostachys bambusoides 'Castillonis' ♀
(Giant timber bamboo)
This cultivar is famed for its golden canes, which are the most colourful of all hardy bamboos. They are thick with deep green grooves, and the leaves are large and lightly variegated. It grows best in hot summers, and its roots are fairly compact in cold areas.

◨ – ◙◊ ✳✳✳
‡ 3.5m (11ft) ↔ indefinite

Phyllostachys nigra ♀
(Black bamboo)
This bamboo has green canes that mature to a solid, shining black, but the plant needs good light to achieve this colour. They are slender and widely branching, and they arch under the weight of the foliage. It is slow-growing and compact in cool gardens, and the roots are inclined to run in warmer gardens.

◨ – ◙◊ ✳✳✳
‡ 3.5m (11ft) ↔ indefinite

PLEIOBLASTUS VARIEGATUS ♀

PHYLLOSTACHYS NIGRA ♀

Pleioblastus auricomus ♀ (syn. Arundinaria auricoma, A. viridistriata, P. viridistriatus)
(Gold-leaved bamboo)
A very popular bamboo with upright, purplish green canes and leaves that are dramatically striped green and bright yellow; the colour is most intense when the canes are cut to the ground each spring. It forms small patches, although it can spread in damp ground. An excellent bamboo for a large tub. P. variegatus ♀ (syn. Arudinaria fortunei, A. variegata, P. fortunei) is a small, bushy bamboo, to 1.5m (5ft), with leaves consistently and cleanly striped with green and white. As for P. auricomis, the foliage is brightest if the plant is trimmed or cut down each spring. The roots are normally compact.

◨ – ◙◊ ✳✳✳
‡ 2m (6ft) ↔ 1.5m (5ft)

Poa chaixii
(Broad-leaved meadow grass)
A most useful grass for woodland and shaded areas, forming vigorous clumps of

SASA VEITCHII

broad and shiny, bright green leaves. The purplish flowers of early summer are held well above the foliage.
◻ – ◼◊ ❋ ❋ ❋
↕ 60–90cm (24–36in)
↔ 45cm (18in)

S

Saccharum ravennae
(Ravenna grass)
Grown for its plumes, which are similar to, but much longer and more slender than, those of pampas grass (*Cortaderia*). It is one of the more outstanding grasses for climates with long, hot summers. A disappointment in cool summer areas, where it is not reliably hardy. It forms large clumps of grey-green leaves to 1.2m (4ft) tall, producing its tall flowerheads above them on stout stems in late summer.
◻◊ ❋ ❋
↕ 4.2m (13ft) ↔ 1.2m (4ft)

Sasa veitchii
(Veitch's bamboo)
The thin canes of this bamboo are purplish green and bear boat-shaped leaves mainly at the tips. The foliage withers to a parchment colour at the margins at the first touch of winter. A highly decorative plant, but it is highly invasive, inclined to escape even when confined in pots. 'Nana' is a dwarf form, growing to half the height.
◻ – ◼◊ ❋ ❋ ❋
↕ 1.5m (5ft) ↔ indefinite

Schizachyrium scoparium
(syn. *Andropogon scoparius*)
(Little bluestem)
A perennial grass from the North American prairies that is prized for its blue-grey leaves, which turn intensely orange-red in autumn and make a valuable contribution to the garden in winter. The tiny, wispy white flowerheads appear from late summer and into autumn. Grow in sharply drained soil.
◻◊ ❋ ❋ ❋
↕ 90cm (36in) ↔ 30cm (12in)

Schoenoplectrus lacustris
subsp. *tabernaemontani*
(Club-rush, Great bulrush)
This huge, clump-forming, rush-like sedge is a native of

SACCHARUM RAVENNAE

SCHOENOPLECTUS LACUSTRIS
SUBSP. TABERNAEMONTANI
'ZEBRINUS'

brackish or fresh waters. The plants are composed of dark green, upright stems, which function as leaves. Recommended cultivars include: 'Albescens', with pure white stems; golden yellow 'Golden Spear', which later turns to green; and 'Zebrinus', with canes alternately banded green and creamy yellow. Grow in fertile, wet soil, or in water up to 30cm (12in) deep. It will grow in both still or slow-moving water.
◻◊ ❋ ❋ ❋
↕ 1.5m (5ft)
↔ 60cm (24in) or more

Semiarundinaria fastuosa ♀
(syn. *Arundinaria fastuosa*)
(Narihira bamboo)
A stiffly upright, stately species, and one of the best garden bamboos. It makes an excellent vertical accent in larger garden displays. The dull green canes are tall and upright, maturing to purple. 'Viridis' is an even taller form with green canes.
◻ – ◼◊ ❋ ❋ ❋
↕ 8m (25ft)
↔ 2m (6ft) or more

Sesleria nitida
(Grey moor grass,
Nest moor grass)
This grass forms low, dense
clumps of evergreen, pale
grey-blue to grey-green leaves.
The whitish, late spring
flowers, held above the
foliage, are black with white
anthers. It prefers neutral
to slightly alkaline soil.
◨ – ◙◊ ✳✳✳
‡↔ 40cm (16in)

Setaria italica
(Foxtail millet)
This annual grass is valued
for its dense flowerheads,
which resemble short
caterpillars thickly covered
with long, silky hairs. The
flowers are followed by grainy
seedheads, and these are
sometimes fed to caged birds.
Sow seed in spring or allow
plants to seed themselves.
◙◊ ✳✳✳
‡ 30cm (12in) ↔ 15cm (6in)

Sorghastrum nutans
(syn. *S. avenaceum*)
(Indian grass, Wood grass)
A perennial grass forming
dense clumps of strongly
upright stems. These bear an

SESLARIA NITIDA

SETARIA ITALICA

abundance of green leaves,
topped by small but showy,
coppery flowerheads from late
summer, which can be cut,
dried, and dyed for indoor
display; the individual flowers
have conspicuous, bright
yellow pollen sacs. Grow in
poor soil, in sun, and protect
from excessive winter wet.
'Sioux Blue' is strongly
upright and has blue leaves,
turning purple in autumn.
◙◊ ✳✳✳
‡ 1.5m (5ft) ↔ 60cm (24in)

Sorghum nigrum
(Black millet)
A large, coarse annual grass
with heads of large, shiny
black seeds in late summer.
Sow under glass early in the
year to give a long growing
season. It is lovely planted
among dusky eupatoriums
and the fading flowerheads
of pink hydrangeas.
◙◊ – ◊ ❂
‡ 90cm (36in) ↔ 60cm (24in)

Spartina pectinata
'Aureomarginata'
(Striped prairie cord grass)
The upright, yellow-edged
foliage of this perennial arches

over gracefully, swaying with
every gust of wind. It forms
clumps or drifts of narrow
leaves, and the reddish brown
flowers are carried well above
the leaves. The roots will run
on damp soils, but this is less
of a problem on average soils.
◨◊ – ◊ ✳✳✳
‡ 1.8m (6ft) ↔ indefinite

Spodiopogon sibiricus
Resembling a bamboo, this
is a clumping perennial grass
with upright stems. These
are set with thin leaves held
almost horizontally, and the
greyish flowers appear in
oval heads above the leaves. It
develops good autumn colour.
Choose a site in light shade;
it will not tolerate drought.
◨ – ◙◊ – ◊ ✳✳✳
‡ 1.2m (4ft) ↔ 1m (3ft)

Sporobolus heterolepis
(Prairie dropseed)
A grass with many virtues
that forms exceptionally dense
mounds of very fine, grey-
green leaves. In summer and
autumn, these are topped by
delicate, fragrant flowerheads,
and large drifts can scent the
surrounding air. The clumps

SPARTINA PECTINATA
'AUREOMARGINATA'

STIPA (FEATHER GRASS)

This is a large genus of perennial grasses, and almost all of them are worth growing in a mixed or shrub border, preferring well-drained soils in full sun. Their attractive flowerheads can be cut and dried for indoor display. The following list is a selection of the best:

S. arundinacea (Pheasant grass) forms mounds to 90cm (36in) tall of thin, khaki-green leaves, which turn orange-brown during late summer; in the wind, they flow like a cornfield. Tiny flowers also make an appearance in late summer on conspicuous, branching, thread-like, claret-coloured stems. The autumn leaves colour best on poor soils.

S. barbata reaches 45cm (18in) tall and is grown for its long, showy awns (feathery appendages to the seeds). The awns can be 20–30cm (8–12in) long

Stipa arundinacea

and are like silken threads at first before they fluff out to their feathery stage. Flowering lasts for about a month above a mound of greyish foliage.

S. calamagrostis makes rounded mounds to 90cm (36in) tall of green foliage. From early summer until the frosts, it continuously produces shaggy, greenish white plumes that turn light brown and sway gracefully in the wind. It is one of the best.

S. capillata is upright with early summer flowers like bunches of silvery, silken needles. They are carried in open, arching heads high above the foliage. To 90cm (36in) tall.

S. gigantea ♀ (Gold oats, Spanish oat grass) is one of the finest of all perennial plants. On stems to 2m (6ft) tall, it bears huge, wide-open heads of glittering bronze

and gilt flowers in the first half of summer; these mature to straw-coloured seedheads and last until winter. The dark green leaves form a low, rounded mound. 'Gold Fontaene' is even taller, to 3m (10ft), with gold flowers.

S. pennata is similar to *S. barbata* but it is smaller and less showy, reaching 30cm (12in) tall.

S. tenuissima (Ponytail grass) is a short-lived perennial grass to 60cm (24in) tall. The leaves are gathered together at the base but splay open at the top like a shaving brush; they are topped with diffuse, much-branched heads of tiny flowers, these emerge jade-green and mature to pale buff. It billows beautifully with every breath of wind and flowers continuously from spring until autumn. It is very finely textured, contrasting beautifully with hard landscape features.

Stipa calamagrostis

Stipa gigantea ♀

tolerate drought and do not die out in the middle, ideal for ground cover. It grows in most soils, but is slow to develop.

🔲 – 🔲◊ ✳ ✳ ✳
↕ 40cm (16in) ↔ 1m (3ft)

T

Typha angustifolia
(Lesser bulrush, Narrow-leaved reedmace, Soft flag)
Bulrushes are coarse and invasive plants of pond margins, producing their flat, upright leaves in two distinct ranks. The dark brown flowers in summer look like velvet sausages, and appear at the tips of the stout, upright stems. Most are too rampant for gardens, but this species is more suitable, since it is less vigorous and is graceful in both leaf and flower. The common bulrush, *T. latifolia*, to 3m (10ft) tall, is only suitable for the margins of large wildlife pools; its rhizome tips puncture most plastic pond liners. *T. latifolia* 'Variegata' is less vigorous with cream-striped leaves. The dwarf reedmace, *T. minima*, is a much smaller, more slender

TYPHA MINIMA

TYPHA LATIFOLIA

plant to 75cm (30in) tall, with round flowerheads. It is the only species suitable for a small pool or tub. Grow all types in water 30–40cm (12–16in) deep, with ample space and depth of mud for the roots. Pick flowerheads of bulrushes early in the season for indoor arrangements; they should be dried, then sealed with a coat of hairspray.

🔲◊ ✳ ✳ ✳
↕ 2m (6ft) ↔ indefinite

U

Uncinia rubra
(Red hook sedge)
This perennial forms low mounds of narrow, v-shaped, tapering leaves, which vary in colour from glowing, dark mahogany red through to brownish green, depending on the amount of light reaching them. Hook sedges resemble their close relatives in the *Carex* genus, but have a tiny hook at the tip of each seed, which assists their dispersal. *U. uncinata* is smaller, and *U. clavata*, the club-headed hook sedge forms dense mounds of dark, evergreen

foliage; its almost black flowerheads on slender stalks are ideal for cutting. All types perform best in relatively damp, well-drained soils, suffering in climates with long and hot, continental summers.

🔲◊ ✳ ✳ ✳
↕ 30cm (12in) ↔ 35cm (14in)

Z

Zea mays
(Maize, Sweetcorn)
An annual grass with long, broad green leaves, which are striped white in 'Variegata', white, yellow, and pink in 'Quadricolor', and red in 'Harlequin'. Flower tassels form at the top of the plant, and showy, edible cobs form in the leaf axils. 'Indian Corn' has cobs with multicoloured grains, 'Strawberry Corn' has burgundy grains, and 'Fiesta' has red, white, blue, and purple grains. For cobs, set the plants out in blocks or groups, not lines. All need the longest growing season possible, so sow seed under glass in midwinter.

🔲◊ – ◊ 🔾
↕ 3.5m (11ft) ↔ 60cm (24in)

UNCINIA RUBRA

INDEX

ACKNOWLEDGMENTS

Picture Research Samantha Nunn
Picture Librarian Romaine Werblow, Richard Dabb
Special photography Peter Anderson
Illustrations Gill Tomblin, Karen Gavin
Index Hilary Bird

Dorling Kindersley would like to thank:
All staff at the RHS, in particular Susanne Mitchell, Karen Wilson, and Barbara Haynes at Vincent Square.

The Royal Horticultural Society
To learn more about the work of the Society, visit the RHS on the internet at **www.rhs.org.uk**. Information offered includes plant news, horticultural events around the country, RHS Plant Finder, a garden finder, international plant registers, results of plant trials, a gardening calendar and monthly topics of interest, publications and membership details.

Photography
The publisher would also like to thank the following for their kind permission to reproduce their photographs:
(key: t=top, c=centre, b=below, l=left, r=right)

Garden Picture Library: Mark Bolton 34bl, 64bl; Eric Crichton 21t; John Glover 10bl, 12b, 20b; Marijke Heuff 15t; Mayer/Le Scanff 6, 9t; John Neubauer 7b; Jerry Pavia 8b; JS Sira 14b, 18br; Rachel White 21cr; Steven Wooster 23b
John Glover: 70bl
Roger Grounds: 65tl, 71bc, 72bl
Clive Nichols: 23tl; Bonita Bulaitis 13t, 30; Hillier Gardens, Hampshire 9b; Lady Farm, Somerset 17br; The Old Vicarage, Norfolk 16b; James Van Sweden 2; Elisabeth Woodhouse 15cl
Photos Horticultural: 64tc, 64br, 70br
Picturesmiths Limited: 41br
Derek St Romaine: 10br, 11tl, 11tr, 17tl, 19tl, 19tr, 22b, 24b, 25tl, 25br, 26clb, 26br, 28cr, 29t, front jacket bl and tl

All other images © Dorling Kindersley.
For further information see:
www.dkimages.com